THE
SOULIFICATI

Secrets of the
SOULAR SYSTEM
and
CONSCIOUS
EVOLUTION

D1528585

BY: LUCIAN BLACK

"Peering through the Cosmic Sphere"

The Adeptus II of the Luciferian Order focuses primarily on the Mental World, the Incipus Degree I on the physical world. This document is designed to offer the Adeptus a structural understanding of the various levels of consciousness at work within the Universe, to a degree.

Herein is no magickal formula, herein is a key to consciousness. Magick is all in the Mind, a sharp mind can execute its magick effectively, accurately and with great ingenuity. The Soulificati peers through the Cosmic Sphere.

Sol Invictus

Published by: Eartherean

Table of Contents

Introduction: ARCANUM DEI   5

Chapter I : NOVUM ORDO ANIMA   18

Chapter II : PLUTOIDIAN   24

Chapter III: NEPTUNIAN   33

Chapter IV: URANIAN   43

Chapter V: SATURNI   49

Chapter VI: JUPITERIAN   58

Chapter VII: MARTIAN   66

Chapter VIII: EARTHEREAN   72

Chapter IX: VENUSIAN   93

Chapter X: MERCURIAN   106

Chapter XI: ANIMA   116

Chapter XII: THE CONSTRUCT   131

Chapter XIII: CONCLUSION   139

OPUS DEI

Herein are not the secrets of the Universe in absoluteness, herein shall be revealed the secrets of the Soular Systems, Conscious Evolution and a Divine Structure of Cosmic Consciousness. For the secrets of the Universe have long been forever veiled in the Light of darkness.

That which is revealed here is only a microcosm of the greatest mysteries, a sacred knowledge that has not yet been exposed to the mind of mankind. This is only a seed of the forbidden fruits of knowledge for this is the knowledge of the Soulificati.

The Soulificati represent the bodies of Light and Intellectual Illumination that exist throughout the universe, in various realms, forms and levels of existence. We are the All, we exist in a complex and multi-dimensional manifestation that is connected via a cosmic neural network that is linked via light waves of all light emitting bodies. Though all are the embodiment of the Soulificati, not all are yet Illuminated, and dark matters still exist.

All things are of Light and consciousness; the Ain Soph Aur, the "Limitless Light". Wherein both higher consciousness and lower consciousness intertwine like a double helix encoding itself with the One Mind. As a trees roots run deep into the darkness of matter, such roots establish a foundation that its branches may stretch forth reaching toward the Light.

The Tree of Life is as much symbolic as it is a realty, for the roots of the Tree of Knowledge reach deeply into the sub-consciousness of the human psyche. These root are a manifestation of a neural network that provides sustenance of the mind and empowers it with the sustainable nutrients for conscious evolution and transcendence.

The Ancient Hermetic's formulated a universal principle "As Above, So Below". That which is of the highest order, is a reflection of that which is of the lowest order. The microcosm is a reflection of the macrocosm and the macrocosm is a reflection of the microcosm. This maxim reveals the truth that the evolution of the smallest simple organism reflects the evolution of the grandest complex organism. Everything is contained within the All. All things are evolving simultaneously as one connected "Construct of Consciousness".

To the Antient Ones, All is mind, All is energy and All is Light. Intelligence ascends into the highest of heavens to only once again descend to the depths of darkness. Pulsating, inhaling, exhaling, expanding, contracting, ascending the highest of highs and descending to the lowest of lows. It is as a waveform vibrating consciousness on all levels, descending to the depths of darkness and matter, and then ascending again to the heights of

Light and Illumination.

For as we ourselves travel this realm shall we find our Self in times of darkness, as well as in times of Light. All of which offer invaluable transcendental experiences towards ascension and then again into descent to return unto an even greater transcendence.

Within the Soulificati, is the path of Illumination and Higher Intelligence, this is the path future gods/goddesses. There is a God Mind present within all of us! A creative intelligence that has the power to manifest itself and influence reality. A God Mind, a Higher Intelligence, a Higher Self encoded within each and every one of us, it is as a nucleus of transcendence. Herein, do not be thwarted by the use of the word "God" we indicate no specific beliefs in regards to this term except a "Higher Intelligence", "Higher Self" and the "Great Architect of the Universe".

To better illustrate the "Mind of All", let's take the human form for example. Imagine if you will, your own human body. Now, take a look at your hand and there you will see a complex structure, a structure that is at your command and bends to your will. If you lifted your hand to look at it, you made it happen. This hand and everyone else's hands are composed of millions of individual living cells that have miraculously bonded their selves together to create the hand. And each cell is held into place by some invisible force that is now under your control.

However, you can only control your hand to the extent that it is designed. You must also understand that it is governed by certain natural forces which you cannot completely control. You cannot make it disappear at will without using an external source to destroy it. You cannot simply think it gone. Your body and mind has been made manifest by some unknown force present, of which you are a construct of this secret force. This Secret Force is prevalent throughout the entire universe. As we travel the path of the Soulificati, you will come to know this secret and the sacred force within the universe, and that all things are composed of pure consciousness.

This Mind Force is omniscient and is composed of millions of atoms, millions of cells, minds, stars, planets, and elements. All of which are bound together within this expansive construct, we know as the universe. A universe which is in actuality a multidimensional multi-verse. All held together by one binding intelligent force. Wherein each living and non-living essence, composed of the prima-materia harnesses its own nucleic mind-force.

This Mind Force, call it what you will, God, the Divine, or whatever name you so choose; regardless of what you name it, it is the Great Hidden Source within All Things. It is true that all things are of this Divine Mind, but only certain entities within the construct have ascended to the degree of becoming creative forces within the universe.

This, degree of influential presence is a measure of consciousness. For some conscious entities possess greater awareness/intelligence, whilst others are of lower/weaker awareness, or frequency.

A being, possessing great strength of this creative force has the ability of governing energies within the universe, and influencing it in great complexity. This same conscious manifestation is also the governing mind-force of your body, your mind-force is the god of its own cellular life form, you! What you are is an initiate within the Bodies of Light known as the Soulificati. Our journey is through the Soular System and toward Anima, for the Sun is the nucleic Mind Force of our inhabiting Solar System.

Remember, "As Above, So Below" for as the nucleus is the center of the atom and orbited by protons and electrons, in like fashion is the sun the nucleus of its Soular System orbited by planets, which are essentially portals. The thought force of the nucleus is the nuclear fusion that creates an attraction that binds the invisible to the visible.

As it is throughout the universe, so too is this mind force ever present here on Earth. Within the Soulificati we are here as Earthereans. We are earth beings, within the ALL. Humankind exists within the Soular System, in the realm of duality and balance. Here we come to know the duality of nature: light and darkness, good and bad, male and female, hot and cold etc..

As Eartheran's we reside in between the realms of war and love, chaos and order. We are here on Earth to assimilate and transcend the dualistic nature of balance and imbalance, especially within our own consciousness. We are readily familiar with this dualistic nature that surrounds us, composed of creative and destructive force which greatly influences the dynamics of the Construct. We have been taught that such forces are either good or evil and that we must choose between the two. However, in truth we are here to reside, accept, and adapt to the center, we are here to balance.

In greater truth, we are to move beyond dualities, for there is no good or evil, there is only, that which is to become. Ebbing and flowing, highs and lows, expanding and contracting, coming into being and extinction. The evolution of energy, the wave form of a dualistic nature. Though some may choose to see it as either good or bad, it is nonetheless balanced in nature and one in purpose. That which is to become is the continued evolution of the Mind-Force and all of its Living Intelligent life forms which are the embodiment of the Construct.

The annihilation or extinction of one thing gives rise to that of another. The old perish and give birth to that which is better apt to advance the

Ultimate Design of the Construct. That which may be deemed as bad may in turn result in that which is good and vice versa. To think one thing is good over another may become the causal result of something one will later perceive as bad.

Therefore, it is more appropriate to be aware of what is correct and that which is incorrect, even then knowing that this too is only perception. Instead know that, that which is to be, regardless, is in essence, transcendence and ascension of the Soulificati. Specimens become manifest and specimens die, all the while the Construct itself manifesting and evolving in greater magnitude than previously established. Therefore, the only measure is what one holds true in ones heart and soul... this is the Light of the Soulificati. This is the creative spark within us that has the power to shape reality. This Knowing that is within us, that is All-Knowing.

The cosmos is a continual ebb and flow of chaos and order, darkness and light, creation and destruction; however, it is of certainty, that All is in Order. Expanding, Contracting, Creating, Destroying, Changing, Growing and forever Becoming Greater. As Above, So Below! The same processes exist within us, at times within ourselves we experience chaos, changing, struggling to grow then finding within us a restructuring, an order to become greater. We are our Self, a reflection of the cosmos.

We should come to realize, that which is perceived as Chaos is merely the restructuring of a New Order evolving. That there is no Darkness. Darkness is a Light not yet perceived. To know that destruction is only the path to clearing the way to creation. Destruction is a process of Creation, the old fades away to give rise to the new. Throughout the cosmos, the process of renewed energies unfold over time, billions of years have passed and billions more remain ahead.

You yourself are made of renewed energy billions of years old, and eventually you too will fade from this Earth. And the energy composed of you and your mind will pass from you to something else and be transformed. You will transcend and become renewed. This energy is borrowed not owned. Energy, Light and Mind is never-ending, it is transformed, and regenerated, renewed.

From the smallest of quarks to the grandest of

galaxies, ALL are composed of the Higher Intelligence, communicating, vibrating and resonating information. The ALL resonating various frequencies, at various levels of the Mind-Force, across the cosmic Construct.

Just as the atom nucleus is encircled by its protons and neutrons, single cell's membrane surrounds its nucleus. Just as the planets orbit the nucleic Sun/Star in its respective solar system, the galaxies spin host to its nucleic core cluster. As Above, So Below. All is in Order, by design and structure! As the ant to the hill, the bee to the hive, the human to the Earth, this is the Order of the Construct of All.

The Soulificati journey through the Soular System, within the Order of the Construct is to develop greater presence, power and purpose. Thereby attaining the realization that we are directly influential to our own evolutionary advancements. Wherein humankind finds the power, presence, and purpose to persevere as we transcend and ascend to the Intellectual Illumination of our Soular System.

Earth is the womb of conscious evolution for humanity within the Soulificati. All the planets within our Soular System are and have been influential in our evolutionary progression up to and toward our current stature of Illumination within the Soulificati.

Through the Soulificati may we come to the knowledge and power that each planet in the Soular System is a sphere of developing consciousness. That each sphere is a portal toward ascension of Intellectual Illumination. That each portal of planetary consciousness remains imbedded within our own conscious. As we climb the ladder and pass through each gate toward ascension. From the darkness of unconsciousness to the Light of Illumination, we the Soulificati travel the path of the Divine Light of Anima.

Herein, is the forbidden knowledge of the gods. Be it known that the path to Illumination begins in the outermost, primordial energies of the Construct of unconsciousness in darkness, further most from the light. As consciousness transcends each phase of evolution as attributed by each planetary portal of our Soular System shall we come closer and closer to Illumination.

We, the Soulificati extend our love and light

throughout the universe, may you travel well and find your way to the Light of Anima.

Chapter I

NOVUM ORDO ANIMA
The Portals of Transcendence

The Sun/Star of the Soluar System is known as "Anima", Latin for Soul/Life-Force. Anima, is the center nucleic Mind-Force of the Soular System known as "Ordo Anima". The Ordo Anima is comprised of the Sun (Anima) and nine commonly known planetary bodies which are the portals to conscious evolution within the Soular System.

The commonly known planets are Pluto (Plutoids), Neptune, Uranus, Saturn, Jupiter, Mars,

Earth, Venus and Mercury. Each planetary body is an attribute of certain distinctive qualities and quantities of energies which we have characterized accordingly. Much of the attributes are classified within the ancient art of Astrology but are in no way limited to this knowledge.

Astrology in its most elemental form of classification is accurate, however, the implementation of astrological forces at play in regards to one's birth month continue to remain ambiguous. The lure of this form of astrological anomaly resides in the propensity of probabilities instead of an exact science.

Astrology in regards to the Zodiac, and Anima's location in the zodiac at the time of one's birth is an arcane science. This science propagates that each sign has a ruling planet and that those born under certain signs, with certain planets, in certain houses are influenced by the attributes of such zodiacal signs.

Let it be known that there is truth within this ancient science in its highest forms, however, the human psyche still has much to learn on this esoteric science. As it is an Art, as much as a

Science, much of it is interpretive and not exact. Therefore here, our focus is on planetary attributes and not the Zodiac.

Therefore, herein the Soulificati we are dedicated to the planetary bodies individually and isolate from Astrology's zodiacal propositions. We will focus primarily on the planetary bodies and their distinguished Mind-Force, and their associated evolutionary consciousness within the Soular System.

Scientifically, all bodies orbiting the Sun (Anima) beyond the orbit of Neptune reside in the realm of primordial energy. That which is on the edge of darkness furthest from the Light force of Anima. The multitude of bodies orbiting the further reaches of Anima represent the unconsciousness being drawn unto the orbit of the Light of Illumination.

Energies circulating the outskirts of the unconscious such as Pluto, Eris, Makemake and other dwarf planets within the Edgeworth–Kuiper belt are the primordial energies of what is known as the underworld, and are referred to herein as Plutoids.

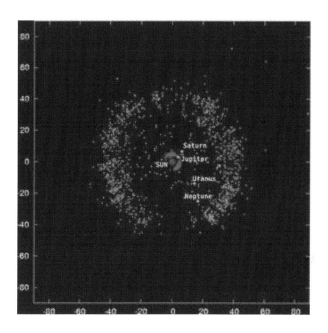

**The Edgeworth–Kuiper belt surrounding Anima,
shown by the green dots surrounding the Ordo Anima.**

The Edgeworth-Kuiper belt creates the outer wall of the Soular Systems cellular structure. The image above provides a visual depiction of this cellular like structure, wherein the Sun (Anima) is the nucleus, of the Soular System. Therefore, the far reaches of the Ordo Anima as shown above creates a cellular like structure that is surrounded by the primordial energies of the underworld, the unconscious drawn toward and seeking conscious by the Light of Illumination.

These outlying energies form the physical enclosure of the Ordo Anima Modus Operandi. These multitude of bodies define the outermost boundaries of the Soular System wherein primordial energies gather on the outskirts of consciousness. Anima attracts primordial unconscious energies that it may itself grow stronger. Anima attracts unconscious energies to itself just as it attracts physical entities and holds them in its orbit.

The Soular System is a representation of an Advanced Construct of the Highest Metaphysical Order of Ascended Consciousness. A Construct governed by the Highest Mind-Force for the advancement of Anima. This same Mind-Force is therefore and thereby operating through each individual consciousness within the Soulificati.

As planetary conscious beings, traveling from realm to realm advancing, ascending and transcending, shall we travel in like fashion from the darkest, outermost, primordial, underworld to the center nucleus of the Radiating Illuminated One. From the underworld of the primordial realm of Plutoids, to the Inner Sanctum of Anima. This is the projected Path and the Portals of Consciousness within the Soulificati.

Herein, is the Path and the Portals of Conscious Evolution, of Transcendence and Apotheosis. That which is revealed herein is the path from Darkness to Light. Journey with us through the portals of Intellectual Illumination, that you may not only see the Light but become the Light, this is the path of Illumination and becoming of thine own Anima, a Source of Light and Illumination with ALL.

As we begin our journey in the underworld, we will transcend each planetary portal and thereby shall our minds embrace the Mind-Force that governs the Soular System and the Soulificati. By so doing shall they who become Bearers of Light, become influential enforcers of the Highest Order.

Chapter II

PLUTOIDIANS
Plutoids: The Underworld

The Plutoidian realm is the realm of what has been called the Underworld or Netherworld. The underworld has been classified differently in various mythologies by many cultures, but all maintain a common underlying theme. The Underworld is typically held to be the place that is beneath the world, primarily the place where departed souls go or simply known as the realm of the dead.

In many cultural belief systems, the netherworld is the place after death from which there is no return. A dark, dismal, torturing of souls, a hell of hells of sorts.

In actuality, the underworld is not the realm of the dead, it is the realm before "Life". It is the residence of energies seeking entrance into the realm of the Living, it is the realm of potential energies, not yet fully kinetic seeking Intellectual Illumination. In many ways have the dead been depicted as wanting to live, in many beliefs, the underworld is considered a hellish place. Prior to the religious doctrine of a lake of fire, the underworld was a dark place, chaotic and lifeless.

Herein is the realm of primordial and unconscious energies. In Greek mythology, the mythological Primordial's were considered the "First Born Ones", though the Grecians had their own pantheon of Primaordial's which included Aether, Hemera, Ananke, Chaos, Cronos, etc., such Primordial's were considered the First Conscious Manifestations that transcended from the darkness of unconsciousness to the Light of Illumination within the Construct.

The Egyptians, Sumerians, Babylonians have all had their own versions of Primordial Gods. This is not new knowledge, this is ancient knowledge, however, the full disclosure has been held secret by the Keepers. The correlative principles between all cultures remains that the Primordial's, were Creation Gods, though some were destructive, they were all revered as the beginning god forms, Mind Forces within the Soular System.

Herein, the Plutoidian realm is the first portal, an entry, birthing realm to consciousness. This realm is as a vast abyss of darkness, unconsciousness but it is not void of consciousness. For there exist potential, primordial energies in a turbulent sea of darkness, attracted to the Light of Anima, the Sun which is the nucleic fusion of Illumination.

Plutoidian unconsciousness acts without intent but is instead motivated by external forces internally. Unconsciousness drawn toward the Light like a moth to the flame, seeking access into the Soular System. Only granted access as needed by an invisible Mind-Force within the Soular System we shall come to know here as the Keepers.

The Keepers are guides within each realm that serve the Lord of Light and are themselves, Lords of Light. The Keepers are representations of conscious blocks, and only they who are deemed worthy and well qualified shall pass through the Portals that lead towards each degree of Intellectual Illumination. All will remain confined and restrained within each respective realm until such passage is granted unto them.

All must stand the test of time, preserver and earnestly seek the Light. As millions of minds evolve toward the Light of Illumination, millions more digress into the darkness or are bound by the thoughts of the realm with which they currently reside. Consciousness may move toward or away from the Light at any time, ascending toward the Light or resending into the darkness.

The Gates to each Portal serves as an entrance as well as an exit. For the portal is reversed for dissention as well as ascension within the Ordo Anima. The Gates swing both ways which allows those who have already ascended to eventually go back as Keepers and/or Guides in that they may advance other souls toward the Light.

As mentioned earlier, the Ordo Anima and its Construct is very much like a cellular structure. As Above, So Below! Much like the egg of the female genus becomes saturated with male spermatozoa, the egg will only allow one chosen sperm to penetrate and fertilize her egg. So too are the outskirts and membrane of the Odro Anima, the netherworld is full of energies seeking entrance into existence. But, only certain, potential energies are granted access into the system and thereby allowed the opportunity to become a higher manifestation within the Soular System.

Evidently the further-most outer edge of the Ordo Anima's gravitational pull resides with the realm of the Primodial's. The Plutoidians are the beginning of conscious evolution. It is the realm of unconsciousness from where all consciousness springs forth. The darkness of unconscious energy and the gravitational pull of potential manifestation.

From the underworld have all here, been born

from. It is not the afterlife it is the darkest portal prior to life. We are all born from a sea of unconsciousness, not yet alive, not yet souls, not yet aware but only a potential energy of the ALL attracted to the central embodiment of the Light.

The Abyss is a sea of soulless entities drawn to the Light of Consciousness. Anima attracts them, calls forth, radiating vibrations with a strong gravitational pull that attracts energy throughout the universe. Anima draws toward itself more and more energy in order to manifest its own greater Light.

The central sun, Soular Light is forever propagating Higher Intelligence within its ranks to manifest more and more Keepers and Lords of Light. Anima is the Soul Center of the Soular System, it is the central intelligence center of the Soular System. From its massiveness and radiance, does it draw from within the darkness potential consciousness from an abyss of unconsciousness.

Fortifying the Keepers and the Lords of Light that potently assist in governing the spheres of conscious evolution and Intellectual Illumination within the Order.

Once a potential energy/entity has been granted access to the Ordo Anima, it is then held and cultivated unto the second sphere, the realm of Neptunians. At this time of acceptance, deciding factors are not so much based on merit as it is on need. Your energy that is you was granted access into the Order based on a need, the only merit weighed was simply a non-biased selection process on intellectual nutrients to the Order, at this time each individual was nothing truly special. Only a potential.

At this stage within the Order, your base energy, which will eventually assimilate into an individual consciousness were granted admission into the Order. This is the seed of the soul which will need to survive and advance itself accordingly or eventually it will be devoured. By some unknown variable or qualification you (as all who were granted access into the Order) have been deemed worthy of traveling through the spheres of consciousness.

The ultimate journey toward the Source of which you were originally attracted and thereby accepted by the Light of Anima. You as all, were attracted unconsciously and granted access by a conscious force much more Intelligent and Aware than you, and granted admittance into a Construct of an even greater Construct in order to transcend through the spheres of consciousness.

The Plutoidian Realm is the first Realm of consciousness, which is unconsciousness. However, as with all realms one must master each dimension before being granted access to the next. Unconsciousness will remain a unknown variable throughout your Conscious Evolution. There are things residing in the unconsciousness that the Higher Consciousness can harness and direct.

The realm of the Plutiodians, is the birth of consciousness from unconsciousness. There are unconscious forces at work within the universe as well as within the Soular System. Being such, there are unconscious forces that govern us at every level of conscious evolution. Magnetism, attraction and repulsion are key element indicators of unconscious forces within us and all things.

That which is Unconscious, does not mean the absence of Conscious, for all things and embodiments are infused with Pure Consciousness. This Plutoidian unconsciousness is the most primordial level of Higher Consciousness that governs the universe and all things in it. Meaning we are unconscious of certain things that may be influencing us, the forces of nature and the universe at large; other individual conscious beings. They exist all around us.

As consciousness journeys forward, into the next realm of the Neptunian subconscious does the Light of Illumination grow stronger and brighter within you and all who ascend beyond the Plutoidian Realm within the Soulificati.

NEPTUNIANS
Neptune: Subconscious

Neptune is the eighth planetary portal from Anima and the second realm from the underworld. Structurally, Neptune is the fourth largest planet in diameter, and the third largest by mass. Noting here: The mass size of a Planetary body is directly proportionate to the Soular Systems conscious dimension. Per se, the larger size of a planetary body the larger conscious block there is, and the greater number of consciousness residing in that sphere. Each conscious realm is directly proportionate to the mass of conscious evolution manifesting within that specific sphere.

The subconscious is a very expansive and powerful force of consciousness. Yet it is very dissipated, erratic and requires the focus of awareness to harness its true power. Accessing the true powers of the subconscious and directing its force will prove a challenge through all portals here to come.

Neptunians reside in the realm of the subconscious. Neptune is portrayed as the Lord of the Sea, riding upon a chariot rising out of the sea pulled by horses. The subconscious mind, much like the unconscious mind is often depicted as a vast sea.

For illustrative purposes, the unconscious is the deepest parts of the abyss where the visible light of the sun does not reach, it is dark, deep waters beneath the surface. The subconscious is between the depths of unconscious and surface of consciousness. The unconscious is a dark abyss; however, know without a doubt the subconscious contains some very lucid qualities.

Neptune is associated with water, the planet itself is believed to be primarily gaseous, with evidence of ice and rocks as its surface. The blue hue is derived from the methane in its atmosphere. Potentially, each chemical and elemental composition of each Planetary sphere may provide a natural habitat for the advancement of conscious evolution upon all realms.

As the Plutoidian realm was a realm of the unconscious soulless abyss, the Neptunian realm is as a lucid subconscious abyss, hidden and lurking beneath the surface of consciousness. The depths of the subconscious, are a watery abyss that is deep and vast. It is the potentiality of All that is, has been or ever will be. It is where all things are possible, a place of dreams and imagination.

However, without consciousness, the subconscious lacks the guiding mind-force to effectively direct itself. The subconscious lacks its own direction at the Neptunian Realm and has no conscious order of its own. It is fluidic and goes with the flow of the tides, flowing effortlessly from one direction to another.

A step up from the underworld, the nether world, the Neptunian realm is akin to the dream world. A place in consciousness where images, visions, symbols, sensations and random apparitions begin taking shape. Within this Realm are they randomly chaotic and randomly ordered. It is the portal where consciousness first experiences, experiences.

The Neputunian Realm of subconsciousness is a difficult depiction. The above image depicts Neptune rising from the watery abyss on his chariot pulled forth from the seas by horses. The horse is a symbol of vitality, a symbol of strong energy and strength.

It represents a strong driving force within us to live, grow, flourish, develop, and to become manifest. In order to evolve there must exist a strong drive within us to become. There must exist a strong psychological and/or emotional state within that is our will to survive, to exist, to become and to ascend to new heights.

This is the subconscious, the realm of dreams and imagination. If Neptunian consciousness were to be associated with brainwaves this would be the level of delta. This is the birth place of ideas rising from the darkest depth of the psyche, however, conscious awareness is needed to navigate this turbulent sea, or else one will remain lost at sea tossed and turned about.

The subconscious is as a vast abyss of randomness. It is where the conscious begins to experience its own illusions of reality. It is the realm of all potential thoughts. The subconscious is the realm beneath the conscious mind that possess all the answers, possibilities and potentialities. Within it is a limitlessness, which has all the power of the Universe to create any potential reality. It is the house of all realities, it is the darkest vision of the

Light of Illumination that holds all potentialities within its womb.

It is here, that your own subconscious had once only a fleeting glimpse of reality, a vision, an idea that captured the Universe and created higher vibrational energy within the realm of the Ordo Anima. And it was this idea, vision, dream of you that was granted access to proceed to the next realm of the Uranians.

Before the subconscious can permeate the conscious, it must first translate the symbolic self into a truth. Therefore, referencing the image above once more, it is worthy to note other symbolic keys contained within this realm.

In the image above, Neptune holds in one hand the orb and in the other hand a trident. He is lifted from the seas of the subconscious upon a chariot, the chariot represents direction, structure and order. The sphere is a representation of solidification and the shaping of perfection. The orb is the manifestation of an idea in perfect form, manifesting itself from the intangible world into the tangible world.

This sphere is a symbolic representation of reality, the two dimensional (circle) brought forth into the third dimension (orb). It is scientifically representative of the nucleic atomic structure, the planets and Anima's form itself. Therefore, the sphere is the symbolic representation of perfection, the orb/sphere is the most perfect formation.

In the opposite hand of Neptune is the Trident Scepter. The trident is the first introduction of conscious evolution unto the three-fold path. The trident is symbolic of the three dimensional realms that are to come as one progresses through the realms of the Soulificati. It is the representation of Birth, Life, and Death. Beginning, Middle, and End. The Mind, Body, and Soul. The past, present and future. The Trident is indicative of a sharp direction, the three-fold mind force that is keenly honed through awareness. It is symbolic of consciousness directing its energies in order to manifest that energy which invigorates and drives the potentiality of a rising conscious manifestation.

Therefore, on the path of conscious evolution the coming of a sentient being must embrace the reality of a beginning, a middle and an end, it must attain direction. The subconscious must take hold of space and time prior to advancing toward the next level of manifestation, within the sphere of Uranians.

Some remaining key figures which are essential elements to the ascension of consciousness. Referencing the previous image once again, the female forms are representative of the intuitive aspects of the sub-consciousness. For the intuition itself arises from the seas of emotions.

The subconscious greatly influences the conscious and the emotions are greatly influenced by the subconscious. In the higher realms where Awareness and Intelligence reign, the powerful influences of the emotions and subconscious are governed and controlled to their greatest potential.

Also within the image are child-like figures which allude to the curiosity and playful energy of youth. Wherein one aspect of our youth has taken flight, and is free, whilst another aspect of our youth grabs the reigns of the horses, harnessing vitality. There is a powerful innocence in childlike curiosity and imagination, to let ourselves fly free and soar without fear. To let go and release control to our inner childlike consciousness to guide us on our journey. We should never lose sight of our inner child, but in order to master consciousness, they will require some discipline which is to eventually come as we progress.

Another essential element is contained within the final figure that must be recognized and embraced. It is the devilish figure blowing into a conch-like shell. The conch has in many cultures been used as a musical instrument, a horn to announce the "coming of". Therefore, symbolically in this image, the devilish spirit (perhaps that which once held you back and have now overcome) announces the coming of a new consciousness from the depths of the subconscious. Announcing, another has arisen!

The announcement of your ascension as a coming of conscious manifestation on the way to Anima has been heard. Your presence creates a vibration throughout the Soular System, growing stronger and more powerful with each passing realm. All vibrations emit a harmonic sound, which is rhythmic. The whole Universe is in rhythm, there is music and music resonates throughout the cosmos. There is a harmony and symphony of the souls wherein everything vibrates. And every manifestation including you possess a unique vibrational pattern. The unique pattern that is your own is of its own frequency, and it is this frequency that will become your own radiant Light as your frequency heightens.

Being deemed worthy and well qualified one may pass through the gates once more into Higher Consciousness. Your journey continues to the realm of consciousness with Uranians.

As with all consciousness, your own consciousness was born from the abyss of the subconscious. And upon your chariot of Light you bring with you the sound of your soul, your own unique rhythm, your vision, your dream, your Light. You have been infused with an ideal that is your soul, a spark. As you have been of your own accord made manifest, let now your initiation truly begin within the Soulificati. Let the Initiation begin!

Chapter IV

URANIANS
Uranus: Conscious Initiation

Uranus is the seventh portal from Animus. Uranus and Neptune are very close in composition and are unique from the other gaseous giants of Saturn and Jupiter. Being that Neptune (Subconscious) and Uranus (Conscious) are very similar in composition also indicates the two are tightly intertwined.

In mythos, Uranus was a god of the heavens or more appropriately the sky and often associated with moisture and rain. The sky, or Air is often seen as a universal power or pure substance. It is the breath of Life, to aspire, inspire and is of the Spirit. Air is often associated with Intelligence. Intelligence is itself the universal power and pure substance.

Air with the inclusion of moisture/water, indicates that the Intelligence holds within it the fluidic element of the subconscious. Correspondences with air are that of the mind, intellect and consciousness.

Entrance into the portal of Uranus is the birth of consciousness from the seas of the subconscious. The subconscious born into formation with the direction and guiding principles of directed thought processes. However, upon this sphere there is no "I" yet, there is no sense of identity or individuality. Herein is only consciousness at work. You exist as you but you are not aware of who or what you are. You have not attained the realization of self-awareness, your consciousness has only thus far been infused with a direction, purpose and/or intent.

Here you are conscious but not aware of self.

Per se, it is as an atom or a cell. There exist at this level of being magnetism and subconscious at this level, there is a purpose but there is not individual choice. All energy is composed of intelligence be it conscious or unconscious, but not all energy/intelligence has intent. It is upon the realm of Uranus where consciousness takes shape, it is the orb from which Neptune delivers from the depths of the subconscious. As previously mentioned, the subconscious delivers visions, dreams, ideas, and insights. This is not to imply that such, are of your own individuality at this stage, for that is to come later upon another Portal. At this realm the vision is that of Anima, infused into a separate cellular intelligence which is being shaped and evolving into a Soul.

Upon the realm of Uranus, the seeds of consciousness are harvested to be brought forth unto the realm of Saturn. Upon Uranus, consciousness is coded to the DNA of the Ordo Anima.

To best understand the portal of Uranian consciousness we must attribute this realm to that of

DNA, creating consciousness with a code/intent. Anima is of Higher Intelligence and the Ordo Anima is a very sophisticated and a highly structured system. Highly structured systems require a code of conduct. It is the realm of Uranians where consciousness is encoded with purpose and infused with essence. There is not a physical strand of DNA, however the concept of encoded consciousness is key.

Essence is defined as: the intrinsic nature or indispensable quality of something, esp. something abstract, that determines its character. Character here refers to characterization, and ideally classification. Here on the realm of Uranus, consciousness is defined, it is here that intelligence is classified. Consciousness is born and upon this birth it is encoded with an essence that is in accordance with the Ordo Anima.

This essence is the root of the soul, the vitality, the spirit and the nature that every living soul consciousness will manifest within the Ordo Anima. All of which is the core consciousness of the future of all coming souls.

Uranian consciousness is the level of

consciousness where intelligence is classified and systematic. It is here that consciousness is infused with spirit, and inspired to manifest itself within the Ordo Anima. It is the Initiation of Isolate Intelligence to become. There are times in life, even at the level we are now upon; the Eartherean Realm, where we are conscious and yet just find our-self going through the motions almost autonomously. We can at times be automated, doing what is expected of us, going with the flow. It is here that you are neither aware nor unaware. You simply are being and acting accordingly.

During such times, there is no sense of identity, no self-awareness. We are as an ant, following the chemical trails, serving without question the hive, following the herd doing without thought that which we are designed to do. There is no fault in this, but in order to ascend and transcend, self-awareness must be harnessed. Otherwise, you are merely acting upon your own base design to belong, feed, reproduce, react and survive. All of which are pertinent in order for consciousness to evolve. However, through the initiation of the Soulificati each and every one of us must come into a realization of a purpose and intent to proceed through the Realms.

When performing menial or rote tasks, our consciousness is like a software program controlling the body like a machine. We are operating on auto-pilot. This level is a prerequisite of Higher Consciousness. It is of a beneficial nature to be able to perform such actions mechanically without thought, but there is no sense of identity, no intent and no power. There is a presence at work within us and all things, which drives us and forces us into action. The intent is not of our own, but of Anima at this stage of consciousness.

Not only is consciousness at this level driven purely to act without question, it is primarily reactive and not proactive. At this stage, consciousness simply responds to external stimuli based on its design, nature and programming. It is mindlessly driven to support its respective environment and reactive to other consciousness.

As we leave the portal of the Uranians, we continue to come to know our soul, our place, intent and power within the Soular System. Initiation continues as we transcend to the next level, the portal of the Saturni, it is here that you will come to know your place.

Chapter V

SATURNI
Saturn: Conformity

Lo and behold, for thou hath entered the realm of time, order and conformity. Here conscious in introduced to the structure of obedience, rules, limitations and regulations. It is here that thy consciousness was brought under control. It is here that you came to know time and structure. It was not of ones own means that such control was dictated, for consciousness at this level is inadequate. It was and still is in need of external guidance and discipline.

Behold, Saturni! Conform! Abide! There is no will except that of the structure, the will of Anima. There is no choice of thy own free will and accord. It is in the realm of the Saturni that thy consciousness is externally controlled by the system, much like Uranian but of a greater design and purpose. Thy will here is the will of the organism, the collective, the will of the institution, the Construct. Your soul is not yet its own energy, it belongs to the higher order, the divine authority.

The transition from Uranian to Saturni is that conscious has come to an identity of "I", but belonging to the structure. Herein, consciousness is as the cell to the body, the ant to the hill, the bee to the hive, the primate to the clan. Here you have attained a limited self-awareness, but it is here that you have a greater degree of awareness within your place, in the confines of the system.

Saturn is the disciplinary, controller, dictator and general. He is often seen carrying a reaper, for Saturn is known as the harvester. This association coincides with Saturn and Cronus, time. In the unconsciousness of the Plutoidians, the sub consciousness of the Neptunians and the consciousness of the Uranians, there is no sense of time and order. Prior to Saturni, consciousness has no awareness of structure. It is within the portal of Saturni, that our consciousness is taught the constraints of time and the rules of order.

It is the realm of Saturn to infuse into the consciousness a sense of time and duty. Consciousness is energy, and energy at work is beneficent to the Ordo Anima and the Construct. Everything is composed of energy and consciousness, even the unconscious is potential consciousness.

The millions of cells that make up your body are all conscious, yet they are conscious only of what they are designed to do. Their work. It is their duty to maintain your organism, just as it is your duty to maintain the structure of the Soular System.

Saturn is possibly the least favorite ideal of conscious evolution, for Saturn is representative of a strict disciplinary figure that shapes us into model citizens of the cosmos. The disciplinary that demands order and conformity of the masses. The Saturni consciousness can be readily witnessed upon the Eartherean realm as the masses have a sense of self but identify it on their place in society, often controlled by the mind of their respective clan or tribe.

Saturn is often depicted as an older male figure holding a child, and in some images Saturn is shown eating the flesh of a child. This is not a horrific characterization of Saturn as a wicked wizard, in as much as an undesired master of structure and time. More appropriately, Saturn takes within itself, youthful consciousness to teach it of its lessons. In the Realm of Saturni, we abide to the construct and the will of higher consciousness. This is the level of consciousness that succumbs to a higher order and has no awareness of overruling it nor disobeying it.

Saturn is a teacher of rules, laws and codes of conduct. In much the same way a parent takes upon their self to teach and guide their own children on how to behave and act within the Eartherean realm. Saturn is the realm of behavioral awareness. All consciousness born must be instructed in the ways of structure and order before they are granted passage to the coming realms of Illumination and godliness.

Saturni is hierarchal consciousness and behavioral modification to fit within a specific structural system. Though Saturn's hierarchal system may infuse a sense of rebellion for some there is no refusal to comply. Regardless, Saturn governs this realm and no one passes through the gates to Jupiter without Saturn's authorization. Without the installment of discipline, duty and responsibility, higher forms of Self Awareness shall not be attained nor granted.

Each living being composed of life and/or mind force from Saturn to Anima, have rightly so been inducted with the essential call of duty deeply infused within their consciousness. Doubt this not, that every living being no matter how they may seem otherwise is committed to a sense of duty in some form. Be it someone in the armed forces to their country, a thug to his gang, a parent to their child, a monkey to the clan, a sheep to the herd, a wolf to the pack, a bee to the hive, an ant to the hill and even an earthworm to the earth.

All things are infused with a sense of duty. Even the rebellious against governments are infused with a sense of duty. They have a sense of duty to their cause, and the peers who are of similar philosophy of reform and/or anarchy.

There is within all a conformity to the Higher Order. We must come to know, that which is your own sense of duty, is in fact a deeper sense of duty encoded and conditioned within us. If it is that you feel not a sense of duty, trust that it is the result of your own deficiency of believing in yourself that is leading you nowhere of importance.

All consciousness has a calling, it is programmed as such, no matter how you dissect it, deep within you and each and every Soulificati is a design, a purpose and a duty. Come to know and understand the importance of structure and Order, revere that which you are made to be within the Ordo Anima.

As previously stated, order, structure, duty and purpose are highly revered principles within the Soular System. Let not the ideals of conformity trouble you. Conformity is required to a certain degree within the Soulificati as it is in the higher and lower realms of existence. There exist certain laws of the universe and certain laws of nature with which we are designed to abide.

Within the universe, there is much freedom within the boundaries of limitations, everything is possible. For example, we must eat in order to live but you have the freedom to eat whatever you please and with whomever you so choose. Are we conforming by living in houses, yes but you can choose to live below or above your means, and you can choose where to live and how to live. Is it conforming to abide by the laws of the land of which you reside? Yes, but you can move to another land with different laws if you so choose.

Understand, that the design of the structure is a beneficent law, it is designed to eliminate the weak and sustain the strong. Unfortunately, humankind has developed laws which enable the weak and lazy, this is not the law of nature. It is man's rules that unfortunately reward the weak and burden the strong.

Saturn has ruled within your consciousness, trained you to conform to the normality of your clansmen, state and country. However, that which was normal one hundred years ago, is not normal today. Things change, you have the freedom to choose that which you will conform to, just as you have the ability to choose that which you feel is your call of duty.

Now that you have shown a remarkable ability to conform, shown that deep within you is a sense of duty and you have verified you are worthy and well qualified within the structure, the time has now come for you to once again transcend. The portal has opened to you, you have left many behind for you have shown potential.

We, the Keepers, of the Soulificati welcome you to the realm of Jupiter, it is here that your sense of Self Awareness will shine even brighter!

JUPITERIANS
Jupiter: Ruler of gods, Self-Awareness

Jupiter is the largest of all planets within the Soular System and was highly revered by many prominent past civilizations. Jupiter as a God was widely worshipped by the Romans and was also revered by the Grecians, as Zeus. Jupiter was and is a super powerful Mind-Force within the Ordo Anima.

Jupiter has always been associated with prosperity, growth, expansion and good fortune. Jupiter is the representation of the Ruling Class, and is the realm of Self Awareness. This is the realm where consciousness is infused with "I". A consciousness that proclaims "I am", "I can", "I will", "I exist" and "I am important".

Astronomically, Jupiter is the largest planet in the Soular System and the fifth portal from Anima. As such, Jupiter's realm remains the realm where the highest level of conscious evolution resides within the Soulificati (to exclude the Sun itself). Jupiterians are of Self-importance, Self-indulgent and is the realm of Self Consciousness.

With the infusion of consciousness coming to the realization that it is conscious, greater complexity of energies are harnessed. Jupiter is the spectrum of intelligence that is self-encompassing, selfish and also limited in the fundamentals of its own ego. It is here that consciousness takes on the desire to power, to control, own and manipulate energies to indulge itself.

Herein, the conscious mind learns the idea of mine. I have, I have not, they have, and I have not.

I want. I need.

Jupiter is consciousness that rises above the system, the conformity and the rules to discover what it needs for itself. Herein, is established a sense of individuality. Herein, is established individual, isolated intelligence within cosmic consciousness, yet driven by primitive instincts and self-perceived needs.

At this Jupiterian level of consciousness, we

are infused with a sense of self, self-importance, self-sustainability and self-preservation. This form of consciousness is slightly higher than the Saturni consciousness, being that Saturni consciousness abides to self-preservation as an instinctive defense, doing what it does only because its instinct is to feed, to breed, to flee or to avoid harm. Jupiterian conscious also is driven instinctively however, this level of consciousness seeks to rise above others, to validate itself and to fulfill its self-importance.

Jupiterians consciousness is Self-Aware, becoming ever aware of its needs and also its wants and desires. Herein is self-serviant. It is here a growing awareness that it is a potential part of the Mind-Force, but it has distinct thoughts about itself and the role of itself in the world. It is productive toward self-gain and seeks stature.

Not only is the realm of Jupiterians self-aware, this is the level of being aware of others as well. It is the consciousness that compares ones-self to others, coming to know where its stature is amongst other, and through this self-comparison seeks for itself its own well-being and success. It seeks stature and seeks to be better than others. It is here on Jupiter that the drive to survive becomes greater than just having basic needs, it is here that the drive is focused on having more than it needs. It is elitist and alpha in nature but has yet to assert itself completely. It is a sense of power and stature that the consciousness of Jupiterians seek.

Regardless to what degree, Jupiter instills within us a sense of being special, important and better than others. It is a necessary, inherent survival mechanism.

In ancient mythology, it was believed that certain gods, especially gods like Zeus, would come down and copulate with humans, infusing their powers into humanity. Therefore, symbolically it is appropriately relative to the Jupiterian portal that consciousness is infused with the godlike consciousness of "I am".

Likewise, this consciousness infused with godlike powers of perception also acquires greater strength. It has the potential to become a more potent presence and a greater force by harnessing a higher capacity of Mind-Force within the Soular System.

As consciousness develops in the realm of Jupiter, it experiences greater levels of pleasure, pain, love, lust, hate and rage. Such forces are conjured up within the psyche to direct the consciousness into action or non-action. The psyche becomes more powerful and present, its desires for itself become very strong. Such forces within the psyche can or will destroy itself or expand itself.

As Jupiterians, the primary force at work is strength and personal power. Anima requires and demands strength, not weakness. Strength progresses, whilst weakness regresses. Therefore, not only is consciousness infused with self-awareness, it is challenged to become stronger, to take a stronghold of itself before it is granted access to the next portal of Mars.

The portal of Jupiter indicates a consciousness that is empowered unto a sense of Self Ruling. The initiation of the Soulificati understands this level of human nature within its own kind. This phase of Self-Empowerment through the coming portal will transcend to Mastery of Self. With still yet a long journey ahead, the soul must become self-empowered, it must be strong and it must have a strong sense of Self to persevere the coming portals.

Without a strong sense of Self-Awareness, self-importance and self-dominance the soul will not endure the hardships to come in order to find its power, its presence and peace. Though many uninitiated will declare such a person as selfish, we must see through our own intentions and become Self-Centered. In a coming portal shall we master balance and therefore be not swayed, nor doubt or fear who we really are to become.

It is within the Jupitarian consciousness, that a sense of identity is developed within our own consciousness. A certain degree of individual personality and characteristic of one's own nature is realized. It is a strong motivating influence in our decisions and actions in the coming portals and will also eventually have to be disciplined. For in the coming portals will it need to be developed and then be tamed.

It is the taming of the ego that will need to be addressed before reaching the Light of Anima. For as the ego is developed stronger in order to survive, it will not be what takes us to the Light. What will take us to the Heart of Anima's Light is a certain knowing, a confidence and sense of self assurance developed within, that we have been chosen.

Take hold of your Self-Awareness and embrace a strong sense of self as you travel on from here. Your ego will, or shall we say must come into check in a future portal, but for the Jupiterian Consciousness and the Martian Consciousness, the ego will serve one well. In the next realm of Mars it will be needed to survive and move forward closer to the Light of Anima. Brothers and sisters of the Light, you having been found worthy and well qualified now have access to the next portal of Mars. Take what you have learned thus far, for the next portal will require you to be strong, mentally, physically and spiritually.

Chapter VII

MARTIANS
Mars: War/Aggression/Assertion

The planet Mars is commonly referred to as the Red Planet. It is the fourth portal from Anima and is often attributed to the God of War. Its red color, that of Iron is often synonymous with bloodshed. The key component with the Martian consciousness is Self-Assertion.

As the soul has been infused with Self-Awareness at the Jupiterian level, at the Martian level, it is now imbued to assert itself, survive and fight for itself and what it believes in. The terrain of Mars, is the preparation of self-affirmation and self-declaration. At this level of manifestation, the consciousness is forced to fight for survival.

The portal of Mars is not just about strength and brutality, but also about skilled combat and intellectual strategy. It represents the capacity to fight for and protect that which we believe in. Again, the previously encoded sense of duty herein comes into play from previous portals, therefore the fight might not just be for one's own cause, but for the cause of something other than one's own desires.

Therefore the Martian consciousness is coming to the realization of one's Individual Intelligence and the role of Self in the greater scheme of things. This role and/or duty embedded within ones soul may be fighting for a higher cause or fighting for one's own cause. A sense of duty to something greater than one's self such as the greater good of all, or the good of one's own sense of purpose.

The Martian Realm is highly assertive and it is here that consciousness may feed also upon the conscious energies of others to maintain itself. It is here on the Martian realm that we consume other energies to nourish and sustain our own existence. It is here that consciousness asserts itself onto others and one is being asserted upon as well. In previous portals, it was the will of the organism, the collective and/or the will of the clan to which we gave duty. We were in essence a slave to the will of something greater than our self.

Upon the Jupiterian portal we came to the realization of self-importance, self-awareness and self-indulgence. Upon the Martian portal we enter a stage of awareness that is more Self-Centered.

We have attained during these portals an identity of self-consciousness. From the consciousness of the lower base desires and instincts to the higher planes of self-awareness, identity, purpose and self-empowerment develop within us. However, in order to assert our own will, we should first know that which is within our soul so that we may be nothing else but true to ourself.

We arise from the whirlpool of unconsciousness to that of self-preservation, to now reside in consciousness that has evolved itself in a way that it now has the power to assert itself within the Soular System.

Though the Portal of Mars is the level of adept consciousness asserting itself, we should understand that this is not altogether negative, it simply is a state of self-progressiveness.

Indeed, upon the realm of Mars, it is a very much a war-like mindset. Mars is consciousness battling consciousness for not only survival, but also for gratification, progression and purpose. This is on the level of strategy and intellectual sharpness for the acquirement of self importance.

One may choose to seek self importance in a greater cause or one may seek self importance of an individual ego-centric nature. Regardless, this level of consciousness reside in battlefield of becoming.

One must take up arms and defend itself, fight for its survival, battle and as a result of being true to ones self, confront the adversity of conformity, laws and rulers. It is within the battle fields of Mars that we fight till our death for that which we believe, and that which we believe is rooted in the essence of the soul.

Also, duly noted here, it is not unusual for like minds to band together and take up arms together to wage war upon other groups that oppose us. Be it we find in our self the need to fight for love, hate, money, food, peace or power; we fight for that which we believe, and that which we believe deep within our soul is that which is individually encoded within us.

There is indeed a difference in assertive and aggressive. Aggressiveness is usually attributed to a negative energy; combative, destructive, intrusive and threatening. Whilst Assertiveness is more of a positive energy; confident, decisive, insistent and strong-willed. When the rawness of aggression is transformed into assertiveness, one can then move forward to the next realm of Eartherean.

However, assertiveness can easily return to aggression as anger may surface within as our attempts to be assertive are thwarted and defused by others who do not support us and have their own agendas. This does not mean what they want is more important than what you want, however, it does mean that if you lose, the other fight was greater than your own. Therefore the coming realms will assist you in balancing out your conflicting nature, that you may know that which you have been encoded with is love. A love for what you are, who you are, and what you stand for.

In the next realm of Earthereans, you will be home, for now, therefore, shall we now grant you access to the portal of Earth, here shall you find a balance of duality and the way of civility.

Chapter VIII

EARTHEREAN
Earth: Peace and Balance

If you are reading this book, it is highly probable you are currently residing within the realm of Eartherean, which basically means you reside on planet Earth. We congratulate you for having made it thus far, however, there still remains a great distance for you to traverse.

It is definite the Earth is unlike any other planet in the Soular System, yet this can be said also about each and every other planet in the Soular System as well. Indeed Earth is very unique, for she is our home planet and a beautiful masterpiece of living consciousness. She is the womb of conscious evolution and has long been revered as our Mother.

It is in her nature to provide the necessary resources to sustain and nurture the life of the creatures that dwell upon her fertile soils. Earth in its present state can be a magnificent paradise providing all the nutrients for a happy and prosperous journey but at the same time can be a tormenting tundra of trials and tribulations. The Earth portal provides its own survival and evolutionary quintessence and she is teeming with life and living consciousness.

As with every portal up to the Eartheran realm, and every portal beyond Earth, it is ALL about survival, more importantly it is about adapting and evolving higher levels of consciousness throughout the gates of conscious evolution. Therefore it is ALL MIND. Each portal is itself transcendent from one state of consciousness toward a higher state of consciousness with the ultimate goal of "Intellectual Illumination" within the Soulificati.

Each being is a conscious evolutionary being

continually adapting to higher levels of manifestation, and each portal the total sum of the consciousness within it. Where once your own consciousness floated in the seas of the subconscious, it grew to conform to the normality of its organism, and to eventually reach the level of asserting its own self, its own intent beyond mere survival. It was necessary for consciousness to develop within itself the ability to be more than just aggressive it must develop within itself the capacity to assert its own will before transcending to the next level.

We know that all of the previous portals of consciousness are prevelant here on Earth, we know unconsciousness, we experience sub-consciousness, we sense consciousness, our own consciousness, we can see conformity at work within our tribes, countries and organizations. We can see in others and our-self self-importance, self-fulfilling consciousness, aggression, assertiveness, etc. etc.

However, herein upon the realm of Earth, the consciousness is initiated to the higher constructs of its own dualistic nature, the balance of dualities and within this understanding of balance shall we develop a sense of peace within itself.

Where upon the portal of Saturn consciousness was admonished to conform, it was preparation for a higher understanding of this nature and its laws set forth within the truth of colonization. In the realm of lower life forms such as bacteria it is about colonization, however, in the Eartherean portal we take colonization to a higher degree of awareness and are thereby initialized into the consciousness of civilization, that we may live among each other in peace and thrive.

It is said that civilization is the most advanced form of social development. Upon Earth, humanity is far more advanced by its civilization than any other colonization of any other creature. Our primitive ancestors formed clans and pacts, wherein there was a dominant Alpha that lead and ruled. And certainly, our species has evolved for over thousands of years on Earth and we have become greatly civilized today in comparison to our barbaric ancestors. However, today more advanced we may be, the alpha domination inherent within our psyche itself has evolved to a greater complexity as well and is ever present on vastly more complex levels of consciousness.

We can easily see within our social system an order and a chaos. Some of us, have a strong sense of Saturni consciousness and adapt and conform to the institutionalized mentality, the Alpha within those of Saturni conformity is not strong, but dormant. Others harbor within a much greater Martian consciousness and to sustain a sense of their own Alpha become highly aggressive to protect their insecurities. They strive to create conflict within the order and amongst the ranks as they attempt to secure their own sense of importance and self validation.

Upon the Eartherean realm, dominance is prevalent on every level of existence; it is the residual energies from Jupiterian "I am important" and Mars assertive powers encoded within us.

It has been said that only the strong survive and this is true in part, but more importantly, it is the adaptability of an organism that ensures the success of a species survival. Encoded within our DNA is more than just genetics, encoded within us is a living consciousness. And at this level we continue to maintain a sense of importance, for this sense of self importance is necessary for the motivation of survival.

Know that a sense of self-importance is essential to survival and self-preservation. Indeed it is very basic primitive self preservation, as well as Higher Intelligence. As Above, So Below!

The objective on the physical plane of Earth is survival, everyone everywhere is seeking dominance, and self-importance at various levels.

The objective of the spiritual plane on Earth is cultivating within a sense of peace and balance within ourselves and within others.

Civilization evolves as our own collective consciousness evolves. Where once our clansmen demanded strength, vitality and a contribution to the clan, this is no longer the case. Today's social structure supports the inadequate and total lack of contributions by weak minded people. We tolerate temper tantrums, entitlement and inferiority as acceptable. We take from those who work and contribute and give to those who do nothing nor provide any value to the advancement of our species.

This tactic of protecting the weak make the weak even more dependent as they leech from the strong, who they think can protect them. When in truth they are imprisoned, controlled and maintained within the system.

In due time we shall witness more and more civilized people moving away from the domination nation and seeking peace within their own self to transcend this primitive infrastructure of hierarchy. There will come a time in the distant future when the people will become Self-Sovereign and be able to effectively rule themselves.

Here on Earth, we sit on the fence of an evolutionary consciousness that will take us collectively to the next level. On one side we come to know and understand this primitive nature within ourselves. On the other side of the fence we see the freedom of conscious explorations of such limited realities. We experience moments of Enlightenment and Illumination within our self and within others that quiet possibly reveal within our conscious as a true capacity for self-sovereignty.

Indeed, Eartherean consciousness is capable of understanding the dualistic nature of the Soulificati, and the Universe itself. We experience the dualistic nature of Light and Darkness, good and bad, right and wrong, highs and lows, hot and cold, fast and slow and the fostering emotions of love and hate.

In order to pass through the gates of the Eartherean portal unto the next portal of Venus, we must fully encompass within our soul, the purity of love. Venus is love and we will discuss this in the next chapter, but for now the notion of love is not weakness or neediness, it is Divine Love of which we shall come to reveal.

Now in regards to duality, it is the duality within us that unbalances us and withholds peace from within us. Internal Confliction. However, it is a common misconception to think in terms of opposing forces, this opposition is only an illusion. Such things as Love and Hate, Light and Darkness, Life and Death are not opposites in as much as they are amplifications of each other. Hate, we believe is the opposite of Love, when in actuality it is the amplification of a love rejected.

When we hate something (truly hate not dislike), it reveals more that we love something worth fighting for that demands to be acknowledged, respected, protected, justified and/or beloved. The way of hate is the premise of which we come to stand against and/or battle that which is threatening the very thing in which we love. Hate is a form of Love, not the opposite of it, the amplification of love in jeopardy.

Remember, within our consciousness is the war-like, battle minded Mars conscious residual presence within our psyche. To fight.

As an Eartherean, come to understand that it is not hate, it is Love! A love in fear of losing that which it loves. Fear that threatens the very thing we love.

As an Eartherean, upon this plane, consciousness is initiated to find balance, peace and love within itself and all things. This is of course is no easy task, for much of this world succumbs to the Martian consciousness of asserting itself with anger, hate, and war. To assimilate the Martin consciousness and work toward balance, open the mind and open the heart, find the center of the self and see clearly that this is only our fellow Earthereans, fighting for that which they love. Know that if others hate, it is nothing more than their love in jeopardy.

Self-love alone is of a lower nature, however it is not to be overcome, but aligned. A Love that is aligned transcends all space and all time and involves all things.

As mentioned, upon the portal of Earth, we are subjected to the consciousness of duality and comparison. Our minds are acutely aware of male and female, anger and peace, light and darkness, cold and hot, and life and death. To realize ALL of the above are one of the same, and are the varying degrees of attributes within the same property, is to transcend the illusion of duality.

"As Above, so Below" does duality exist? Yes and No. All things are a reflection of All things.

For it only exist in relationship and as a reflection of itself and stands not alone. We see darkness where we do not see light, however, there is light everywhere, it just cannot be seen with the limited perception of our eyes alone. Our eyes are limited in faculty to only see within a limited spectrum, which is known as the "Visible Spectrum". However, we know there exist radio waves, microwaves, x-rays and gamma rays which our eyes see not. But with the right equipment we can see these realms of Light more clearly. Therefore, we know there is Light everywhere, just because we cannot see it, does not mean it does not exist.

Such is the limitations of our perceptions on Earth. There are things here and beyond which we cannot see, hear, smell, taste or touch. Just because we cannot see it, hear it or touch it, does not mean it is not present. Our own cellular devices operate in waves which are invisible to the eye, but with the correct receivers, the devices operate as designed.

For example, a cell phone is sending and receiving electromagnetic waves at this very moment, these waves cannot be seen, cannot not be heard but the devices are equipped to process these unseen light waves. To further support this claim, we can reference various other species on this planet that can process wavelengths that humans cannot.

Though human perception is limited there exist other creatures which can sense much more than humans. For example it is believed that birds, various insects such as bee's, and even dolphins can detect manufactured electromagnetic waves used by human devices. They can do so because their senses are equipped to process higher frequencies which remain invisible to our own senses. These frequencies carry information. As such, visible Light is a specific range of electromagnetic frequency, all electromagnetic waves carry information.

As we progress onward from here toward Anima, we will come to know more of the profound effect and relevance of electromagnetic waves. Specifically, Light within the Soular System and the Universe itself. For Anima, is ever communicating with all entities within the Soular System at various levels of conscious evolution, and consciousness is a receptor of information. The mind of every creature on Earth itself is also emitting and receiving electromagnetic waves continuously, consistently processing internal and external information in the process.

All of which is communication within the

Soulificati at a magnitude and multitude of various levels. Everything is intelligence communicating with everything without everything even truly knowing it as such. There is throughout the universe as well as within the Soular System and to include the planet Earth, Higher Intelligence communicating at every level.

Here on Earth, it is that we are initiated into the balance of dualities in order that we may become ascended civilians of the Soulificati. As an Eartherean, you are an adept within the Soulificati. You have transcended and ascended to higher states of conscious awareness. Yet, here in the realm of Earth we are to harness the dualistic power of singularity. We have the ability to reflect on this, externally as well as internally.

It is here, that we come to know the conflicting nature of duality as the embodiment of one and All. For within our-self, is an internal battle between what we deem opposing forces. It is here upon the Eartherean realm we assimilate this illusion and calm the storm to find peace and power within us, as forces join together and unify the body, mind and soul.

Integration of two into one. We bear witness to this throughout this realm especially at conception. The sperm cell and the egg unite, and cells divide again and again, until there is formed a multicellular organism that is one from the two dualities. And within these multicellular human forms, comes equipped a human brain that is itself one brain consisting of two hemispheres, the right hemisphere and the left hemisphere.

Think it not coincidental the human brain itself is composed of two sides/spheres?

Wherein, it is balanced by certain cognitive functions deemed to be dominated by one side or the other. Research suggest that the left hemisphere is the analytical and verbal hemisphere, while the right hemisphere is the more holistic creative. The Left holding logic and reason, while the right is abstract and creative. Balancing of the two cognitive spheres affords one more agility and ability to maneuver and master this specific realm.

Though the hemispheres are separate, they inevitably work together as one. Earth, in balance is integration. Prior to the Earth portal we were initially collective, then became individual, and now we must integrate who we are individually within the whole of the Soulificati. By doing so we ascend once again to higher consciousness.

Eartherean initiated consciousness has become aware of the dualities of individuality of every element and its existence. We are aware of the masculine and feminine energies in all things. The earth can be both dry and moist, the air can be both sustaining and suffocating, fire can be creative and destructive, and water can be soft and it can be hard. We are aware of each of these elements within our own bodies, within our own consciousness we find the dualistic integration of intelligence and intuition.

Of considerable importance is the prominence of masculine and feminine energies upon the Eartherean realm. Both of which are also present within each portal throughout the Soulificati and the Universe itself. Upon the Eartherean realm, sexual energies play a specific role in all organisms for reproduction and self-replication.

Within each sex, the basic structure of the organism is the same regarding the nervous system, digestion and respiratory systems. It is the reproductive organs that are of primary difference (to include the breast and genitalia for most species). Each body is uniquely different primarily on sexual gender and its respective hormones. However, be it male or female, the chemical composition of the species incorporates both masculine and feminine qualities, and are composed of Yin and Yang energies.

Duly noted, all humans possess both masculine and feminine hormones of testosterone and estrogen at varying levels. Testosterone is prominently higher in men making them more aggressive, hairy and muscular, while estrogen is more prominent in women making them less hairy, shapely, nurturing and fit for reproduction. We can easily determine if a woman has higher levels of testosterone than another woman by observing her features. Strong cheek bones, square jaw, broad shoulders, hairy arms etc. indicate higher levels of testosterone within a female specimen. We can likewise observe a male with more estrogen than other men by accessing his feminine qualities, such as slenderness, soft voice and sensitiveness.

Though our physical structure is either male

or female, men have within them feminine hormones and women have within them masculine hormones. We may appear to be one or the other outwardly, however, we are internally and esoterically of both natures. The same holds true to logical and creative thinking capacities of the brain.

As mentioned earlier, concerning the two hemispheres of the brain, when it comes to intelligence, the functionality of the right and left brain hemispheres will determine if one is more logical or more creative. Both hemispheres however are integrated to balance the thought process. ALL is a collaboration of universal thesis and antithesis, balance and counterbalance. Polarities, positive and negative. Extremes of hot and cold. Projections of attraction and rejection. Processes of creation and destruction. The collaboration of Order and Chaos.

On Earth, we witness the unique alliance of several elements fluctuating in perfect balance and imbalance. Earth, air, fire and water all uniquely different in nature, yet all uniquely integrated to manifest a life sustaining environment here on Earth. These very elements also exist to a varying degree within every living organism on Earth. The human body itself is composed of mostly water, yet the earth gives it substance, it's cellular structure, fire flows through its nervous system to animate it and the air gives it the breathe of life.

The same holds true for all living organisms on earth. All elements composed of each other to foster a multi-cellular organism that is alive, thinking and supportive of the living body of Anima here on Earth. The energy of the Sun animates all life and consciousness throughout the Soular System and is therefore imbedded in all consciousness.

As an Eartherean, the greatest secret of the Soulificati is that all living beings are infused by Soular intelligence. Meaning that all life, at all levels are composed of Higher Intelligence. No matter the degree of conscious evolution within the organism, all are the embodiment of the suns energy and intelligence.

The level of manifestation inferred upon the organism here is dependent substantially upon that beings ability to distinguish its own sense of duty and its own sense of love. Does the cell in the body love the body or is the cell in the body simply driven by design to do that which it does. Does that one cell know it is a part of a larger body and by so knowing it does its best to sustain itself and/or the larger body. Or is the cell driven by design to do exactly as it was designed to do without question or awareness of why it is what it is. Are you yourself at a level of conscious evolution here, upon the Eartherean portal, that knows duty as designed to conform, or knows love as duty?

Indeed, we are basically designed to a degree of conformance, but we are also highly decreed to a "love" of performance! From where does the navigation arise? Is it externally or internally made manifest? Be assured that it is indeed internally coded within us and it is affluently effected by our external environment and conditionings. Just as the unconsciousness of the Plutoids are attracted to the Light of Anima, it is a Force of Love that is calling us toward conscious evolution.

Hereto and hereafter has the Light and Love of Anima been calling unto you and moving you toward greater and greater Light and Love within you and all things. It draws you to it, its gravitation is strong and urges you onward.

As you proceed next unto the portal of the Venusians, love will take on a whole new meaning to your soul. Do not be dismayed, our Love is not weakness nor is it romanticized, our Love is evolutionary and empowering.

Here on Earth are you to find balance, cultivate yourself, refine and distinguish that part of you which is animal and that part of you which is Divine. Rise Above, Know Below. One must embrace, assimilate and integrate the physical form with the Divine.

So it is that your time here is short, and you may possibly have many lives here to come until you have mastered a balanced self-awareness and balanced self-love which is inclusive of a love for All things. For we cannot truly love another until we can love our self . This love of which we speak is not strictly compassion, pity, desire, lust or weakness. It is strength of honor, wonder, dignity and duty within the soul to commit its life, existence and manifestation of itself to the calling of Anima that is within us, our guide, and our Light.

Earth is both a state of abundance and a state of poverty. Poverty is lack and a sense of without, which is a state of mind. Abundance and love are also a state of mind. Live in abundance and in love and surely Anima will favor you. But bear this in mind, abundance is not excessive, gluttonous nor arrogant. It is the abundance of Light and Love that harmonizes and synthesizes every essence of ones being.

Balance, Love, Peace, Knowing, Duty, Honor, Integrity, Civility and Truth. This is the Light of Love, this is the key to the Portal of Venusians.

Transcend any notions of love being a form of weakness, for true Love is true strength. Now is the time to the passage of the Venusians.

Chapter IX

VENUSIANS
Venus: Love and Beauty

Venus, long known as the goddess of love is the second portal from Anima. The name Venus is a Latin noun which means "sexual love". This is not to be confused with lust or mere intercourse, it is more aligned with the experience of a pure pleasure that comes with committing and connecting with not only others but with the universe on a very intimate level. It is also the connection, integration and balance mastered in the Eartherean realm of polarities.

Venusian sex takes sex to a higher level, whereas on a base level it is merely instinctive to procreate, on a mid-level it is lust and desire for another, on a higher level it is a pure connection between two Soular beings. Again, to consider the portal of Venus as purely sexual gratification is in error. There are many levels to love and though sex is inclusive it is not exclusive. Sex as a means for reproduction and/or lust held strong through the realms up until Venus. Wherein, love is a powerful connection even without physical intercourse.

At the level of Venus, everything become integrated by connections. On the Eartherean realm we experienced and valued connection over hate, war and separation. We built and lived upon a sense of community and communion. We thrived on connecting and hated that which threatened these connections.

There are various degrees of love. There is the love that a parent has for their child, this love is true in that this love is a physical bond between two beings, one being born from the other. As the parent, it is encoded within us to protect and provide for the child, therefore it is as much love as it is an innate obligation to ones offspring.

It is our duty to love and raise the child the best we can to make the child suitable to sustain itself, eventually on its own. And as a parent we must sometimes show tough love, we must also punish for wrong doing as we attempt to raise our children on Earth in civility and truth. However, more often than not, does the parent long to hold the child, nurture it, love it and help it grow in the Light.

There is also the love we hold for our brothers and sisters, a love hate relationship at the most, but this love for our siblings is a sense of duty to family. This love runs deeper and we truly care for the well-being of our family members. Such is the love of our parents. As children we are completely dependent on our parents love to guide us and grow us into healthy human beings. This love is an environmental conditioning, as we are conditioned to think certain ways based on our immediate family of which we were raised with. This is at its most base level conformity to the clan out of a love for our own kind.

Through their love, they fed us, nurtured us and guided us. As we grew to adults, the experience they gave us determined how we behaved, acted and will feel as adults. If our parents were not loving parents it will take greater effort for us to be loving parents our self, if at all. If our parents were abusive or negligent so too will we exhibit the same mannerisms of intellectual conditioning.

Our parents and siblings have the greatest impact on our development that begins at a very young age. However, we can as adults can overcome and intentionally change this conditioning. It is more difficult to alter our conditioning patterns than it is to abide without question of why we are like we are. We can if we so choose to, to be different and break the patterns, for we may want to give to our children what we did not have and to also be our self more than what we have been taught to be.

Outside of the family connection, there is a love of other people in general. This form of love is compassion. This compassion is critical to harness in order to pass through to the next gate of Mercury. For we must hold within our hearts a sincere compassion and love for others. We must desire to help them grow sincerely, we must when asked, be there to help and assist others in personal development, especially when it comes to spirituality. The greatest gift we can impart upon our fellow travelers is love and wisdom.

It is no coincidence that the greatest spiritual leaders throughout the ages preach and teach on "Love", true and sincere. For back on Earth, they knew the next level of transcendence is "Love". Though they primarily teach love for one another and also a love of god, so few teach or have taught that we must also have a love of self. We must possess a true love and compassion for our self before we can truly love others. This is not arrogance or vanity. For that which we dislike in others, we dislike in our self. We must come to accept who we are and love who we are, just as we should love others for who and what they are.

However, it is a falsification of love that we must be subservient to others, and we must not always put others before us. To always place others before ourselves has the potentiality to create animosity. By so doing will others take us for granted or take advantage of us. The Love we assimilate as a Venusian is not weakness or neediness. It is empowered and will not allow or permit itself to be taken for granted or our sincerity to be unappreciated or non-reciprocated. This is accomplished through a sincere self love first and foremost.

There will be times as we come to master love, that this will be the case. There will be times when our love is not appreciated or reciprocated. Do not be dismayed, the love of ones self is to know when to withdraw our love and redirect it, toward others who would benefit more from our love. Take heed, that when others demand your love, your sincerity, and do not appreciate this energy, they are essentially only feeding off your energies.

Such people are emotional and psychic vampires, they will drain you of your vitality and leave you feeling drained of energy and life force. As a coming master of love, feed those who are hungry, love those who need it, feed not the greedy of self importance only. For a balanced loving relationship is an elevating experience and should heighten the senses of all involved.

As one comes closer into the possession of a Venusian love, people and animals will be drawn to them and naturally gravitate toward those who possess this energy. Follow your heart, you will know, sense those who are worthy and deserve your love and attention. You will also master an inner knowing that will guide you to give love and light to those who are ready to receive it and evolve from it.

Essentially, love is connection; the greater the love the greater the connection. When we realize that all things are connected through the one Source, we have spiritually (energetically) bonded with all things. It is through this bond, this connection with all things and the energy of everything, are all things made manifest. Always remember, connection is key.

With that said, if there is one way of love that we all should all master other than compassion for others, it is the art of sexuality, the art of making love. Back on Earth, the majority of humans do not fully understand the power of sex. On a primitive and essential level, copulation is primarily for species survival, it is the act of reproduction. Humans are exclusive to the power of sex outside of reproductive reasons. Most all other animals do it for reproduction purposes only, humans have evolved to do it solely for pleasure and for desire.

As consciousness elevates to higher understanding, it attains awareness of greater complexities of base consciousness. For example, a dog is driven by instinct to mate, whereas a human does so with other intentions. So much so, that it can be romantic, perverted, sadistic, ritualistic, and even experienced as divine.

As mentioned earlier, love is connection. Sexual intercourse is greater than a physical connection it is a spiritual connection attained through physical connection. On Earth the level of connection between two or more people on an intimate level heightens sensualities of existence.

The feelings of love and desire invigorates and excites the sensational being. Humans long to be loved. Humans long to feel love. Humans long to feel connected, crave to be wanted. Love is a powerful force within the universe the co-joining of opposites, the copulation of energies. Humans have the capacity to experience it at various levels to include passion, desire, lust, want, need, compassion, tolerance and acceptance. However, at a higher level it is inexplicably, connection.

Throughout your journey from one realm to the next, you have discovered a sense of self-importance and individuality. During the Eartherean initiation, you were admonished to find an internal balance within yourself and within all things. It is during the Venusian initiation you must find your own connection within yourself and with all things. It is time to connect to the All, and to do so we must first connect with Anima. There must be found within yourself a love for all things. From Venusian to the next realm of Mercurians and on to Anima, we shall see that all is a progression of Love and Light.

Be forewarned hitherto: many will find connecting on an intimate level with All things to prove difficult. We shall face our own selfish desires which present a multitude of blocks and locked doors. To open oneself up to Love and Light, to let go and trust in Anima is no easy task. However, if one is to shine and become Illuminated, one must take this path and relinquish all presuppositions and preclusions.

The greatest hindrance of transcendence is our own suppression of who we truly are based on fear and insecurities. Be it that we were programmed at a young age to hide certain things about our self as unacceptable or do so because we have been hurt which is its own hindrance set forth by another to control us. Know that, if we are to transcend we cannot exist in protection mode. We must allow our self to be free to love without fear, we must be free to be our self without self imposed limitations and insecurities.

Therefore the initiation of Love within the realm of Venus is the awareness of connection. This involves a connection with ones self, others, Anima and the universe. This connection within the Higher Order of Anima does not render ones individuality extinct. Instead, one becomes a greater presence in the Higher Order through this realization. Higher Consciousness is of the Highest Order. Find that love that connects you with all things. And know, you are not alone!

As mentioned earlier, love is experienced on various levels of connection. There is self-love that is both self-servient as well as self-love that is selfless. As Above, So Below. For just as we experience self-love so too does Anima experience self-love, for Anima is also conscious of its own self-preservation. In the same manner, can Anima be selfless in its love by giving of itself and of its Light to foster consciousness that grows of its own accord within its own Soular System.

Anima is composed of and operates on Light and Love, it is upon the Eartherean realm that we are introduced to the precepts of love, it is upon the portal of Venus that we will come to master it. Herein do souls become the masters of Love. We must fully understand and master Love before we may transcend to the next realm of Mercerians. In order to do so, we must come in control of our emotions and realize that all is Love. There is no hate, no resentment, no jealousy, nothing but Love. We will then understand that all emotions have their roots in Love and stem from it, the aforementioned are nothing more than the negative projections of love.

Therefore, in order to become more Illuminated and closer to Anima we must come to possess the truth of Love. In possession of the truth of Love, Love is like a radiant fire. As it is closer to the heart and soul of Anima, which itself is pure fire, pure Love, so it is here that our Love is like a fire, a Light. We become brighter, elevated and consumed by Love. Our connection to the universe is infused and enlightened through Love. A love of others, a love of self, a love of all things and a love of the universe, we are a part of it All, and All of it is a part of us.

Within this Love of all things is the ability of consciousness to immediately access higher knowledge through the construct surrounding it. Within all things is a mathematical equation of symmetry, rhythm and design. The secret within this equation is the other aspect of Venusians, which is Beauty. Venus being the realm of Love and Beauty, there exist within these aspects a higher consciousness and awareness of perfection. For beauty is symmetry.

Within nature and within the universe itself there is an equilibrium, harmony and rhythm. We were introduced to this esoteric truth on Earth in relation to balance. Therefore in the realm of the Venusian consciousness we come to the mastery of Love and Beauty. The Venusian conscious is highly aware of the harmony and rhythm within the construct of the Ordo Anima, in nature and throughout the entire cosmos. There is within this construct a harmony and love within all things.

There is a balance and symmetry of the Above in relation to the Below. Both of which are a reflection of the other.

The closer we come to Anima, the brighter we become, the more illuminated and radiant we become, the more brilliant we shine. Love is of a higher level of consciousness, a radiant fire of the Soulificati.

They who are the Masters of Love, move forth to Mercerian Consciousness. Mercerians are those illuminated beings that are the travelers and messengers through the Soular System, harvesting and propagating higher consciousness.

If it be that thou shalt pass this Portal of the Venusians to the Portal of the Mercurians, you have reach a level where your Soul has the power and influence to reach other souls and assist in their ascension toward the Light of Illumination having mastered and attained all the degrees of all other realms of consciousness.

Chapter X

MERCURIANS
Mercury: Messengers

Mercury is the smallest planet within the Ordo Anima, as well as the closest planet to Anima, the Sun. Mercury travels its orbit quickly around the Sun and only takes 88 Earth days to complete one orbital cycle. Its surface is much like the moons and its temperatures vary from 100 K (−173 °C; −280 °F) at night to 700 K (427 °C; 800 °F) during the day. Mercury being the smallest planet in the

Ordo Anima is directly proportionate to the amount of Mercurian consciousness within the Soulificati.

Mercury also known as Quicksilver is an element with a very unique quality. Mercury/Quicksilver in an impressive substance that has a very low freezing point and remains as a liquid that is fluidic, and has a highly reflective, mirror like appearance. The Alchemist of old believed Mercury was the First Matter from which all metals were formed. They believed that the Sulfur contained within Mercury could be used to transform base metals into gold, this transmutation of matter was the Alchemist's goal in the material world.

However, in the spiritual and esoteric world the transmutation process of the metals of lead into gold were actually symbolic of the transmutation of a leaden soul into a golden soul. The science combined physical and spiritual sciences in order to manifest the most coveted item in the alchemical world, the Philosophers Stone.

Mercury as a god was commonly known within several cultures as a Messenger God. Though he has other aspects such as prosperity, his most widely known aspect is that of a traveler and Messenger of the Gods.

The Romans closely associated Mercury with the Greek God Hermes. Hermes is a god of transitions and boundaries; and he moves freely between the worlds of the mortals and the divines. Mercury also is known to be a protector and patron to travelers, especially into the afterlife where he is considered a conductor of souls.

Being a Messenger of the Gods, Mercury/Hermes is closely associated with communication. Such communications associated with Mercury are directly influential with higher awareness, higher intelligence and higher planes of existence within the Ordo Anima. Mercury/Hermes carries with him the Caduceus. The caduceus is often used as symbol within the medical fields and is accurately associated with medicine, however it has a much more ancient divinatory meaning.

The two serpents represent the balance and intertwining of opposites. The serpent is widely associated with knowledge and wisdom, in some cultures the serpent is considered good and in others it is deemed evil. As with knowledge, it is neither good nor evil, it is neutral. It is the intent and use of knowledge that makes it good or bad.

An integrated duality of polarities was mastered during the Eartherean portal. This was essentially an integration of information and knowledge, and herein the two serpents represented dualistic nature of the two hemispheres of the mind and consciousness. With Mercury, the intertwining serpents of the caduceus also implicates the spiraling nature of DNA, the source code of all life, information.

We know, scientifically that DNA contains the knowledge and information stored within which itself is coded for every living thing. This information is carried out through the RNA on every cellular structure to ensure the living structure abides to the code and maintains its form. This too, includes the cellular bodies of each Soular System and every galaxy. Though this information transformation varies in source, frequency and modality; intelligence is transmitted on every level of every being.

Further dissection of the caduceus of Mercury includes the significance of the winged staff. The wings represent the freedom and mobility of the source of intelligence. The staff is a symbol of power in the material world. Mercury was therefore associated with commerce, business and trade. Mercury intelligence is industrious and business like. For to be a messenger one must have effective communication and negotiation skills. Communication is a powerful and critical force within the Soular System, for Anima is the life giving source of all information within is construct.

All the above attributes of Mercury, encompasses a powerful consciousness closely related to Anima. First and foremost, on the Mercurian level of consciousness, all other conscious portals have been succeeded and transcended. The Mercurian is closest to the Sun, and therefore this level of consciousness works intimately with Anima throughout the Soular System.

Indeed, the Light of Anima shines into every portal, pouring forth information into every level of consciousness; and it is the Mercurian Messenger that travels through all portals propagating and guiding souls through the portals closer to the Illumination of Anima.

As a master of all realms, the next level of mastery is the transference of this Higher Consciousness upon all levels of manifestation. Therefore, at this level of consciousness we transfer our own higher states of consciousness upon the lower planes of existence and infuse souls with more Light to help them transcend. The Mercurian's are travelers and messengers into all the realms of consciousness whose purpose is to heighten and elevate consciousness, within ourselves, others and all things throughout the Soular System.

At this level of consciousness do we travel through all the realms, Plutoidian, Neptunian, Uranian, Saturni, Jupitarian, Martian, Eartherean and Venusian.

And in each realm do we bring a message, the information, knowledge, consciousness and awareness of Higher Intelligence throughout each and every realm. Per se, to the Saturni realm of conformity do we bring the coming awareness of Self-Awareness, and to the Jupitarian level do we bring the coming awareness of assertiveness, and self-importance. In each realm the Mercurian's are considered the Guardians or Gatekeepers.

The Mercurians are the Keepers. We hold the keys to the coming realms and are messengers of God, the Source, Anima.

Now that we are dealing directly with consciousness and conscious beings we come to know the influence of communication on various levels of being. As a Mercurian, not only do we travel through the material world but we are conscious energies and beings in the spiritual realms.

Meaning that a Messenger of the Gods, a Mercurian, may be with you right now but you are not be able to see them due to your limited perceptions. Or they could possibly even be inside of you as a part of you, born into you and chose to revisit this realm to grow and help others grow by touching lives one at a time.

Either way, they are speaking to you and/or through you, nudging you and others to higher awareness. Possibly, such messengers can be what humans call angels, and they are here to help you attain higher degrees of intellectual illumination as Guardians, Gatekeepers and Guides if you but only listen to the silent voice within you, you may come to know this voice as your own Higher Consciousness.

In consideration, so too must we address the possibilities of the existence of demons, those beings which are not here to help us ascend but to bring us back down to lower consciousness. Just as there is a strong pull of Anima to draw you to the Light, there is also the unconscious darkness that remains a part of all of us and all things. These energies pull us away from the Light and back into darkness and unconsciousness.

As it is not of intent to define the reality of angels and demons herein, we will only imply that there are forces at work within the construct that are effectively influencing consciousness on higher and lower realms of being. The Mercurian level of consciousness has been infused with Love and Light. Such a being can in no way be associated with evil. Within reality, this level of consciousness has surpassed all concepts of good and evil. At this level, consciousness exist solely for the advancement and ascension of Intellectual Illumination within the Soular System.

For clarification, understand that higher consciousness exist within us, as well as around us. We must understand that consciousness is energy, intelligence is everywhere and in all things. Information is all around us and within us. At higher levels of consciousness can we communicate with higher levels of intelligence within all of manifestation. We have come close to the Light of Anima and our own consciousness is infused by the warmth, the fire, the Light and the Love of Anima.

For we have become vastly Soulular and by

being such, can we transcend all realms and communicate consciously at all levels.

At this level of Mercurian consciousness, we are the messengers of the gods, we are in and of our self, godly. Imbedded within us, is information and sacred knowledge, which are messages to our self and to others. If a Soul is at the level of Mercurian, its capacity to communicate with others, with all other things, living and non-living, and its ability to communicate is highly influential.

We are a proponent of the divine Light of Higher Intelligence. The Mercurians are the closest to Anima that we can be without actually becoming one with Anima. Noting some Mercurians have already become infused with Anima and return now once again to deliver even greater Light unto the Soular System realms. We are to become the Light itself. To become infused with the Light and one with Anima.

Chapter XI

ANIMA: SUN/LIGHT SOURCE
Nucleic Center, Source of Light, Radiant One

*"You who are the source of all power,
whose rays illuminate the world,
illuminate also my heart
so that it too can do your work".*

The Gayatri ("Sun Prayer")

The Sun is the shining star of our Solar System, and it is the most prominent force within the Ordo Anima. It is the nucleic center which radiates the most powerful force in the Soular System and the most potent source for all consciousness and life within the Ordo Anima.

It is the largest object in the Soular System and accounts for about 99.86% of the total mass within the Ordo Anima. The Sun is a nearly perfect sphere of nuclear fusion and estimated to be approximately 4.5 billion years old with approximately 4 billion more years remaining. The Sun is mostly composed of hydrogen and helium and is classified as a yellow dwarf star, but will undergo drastic changes throughout its lifetime as it transforms into a red giant. As a red giant, it will by then consume, the orbital planets of Mercury, Venus and Earth.

Though we may know its physical properties, it does not lessen the true powers inherent by the Sun. The Sun itself is a self-contained manifestation, bearing Light. It is a self sustaining, radiant source of energy, information and Light. It is undeniably the primary source of life sustaining light/energy for Earth, without it, life on Earth would cease to exist. So regardless of its molecular composition, the Sun is a highly prominent and powerful force upon our Eartherean Realm.

Not only does it provide the light of visibility for survival, it also supplies the planet with life sustaining energy to all life forms, plant and animal.

All life is dependent on the suns energy for survival, even the creatures hidden in the depths of darkness, in one way or another absorb some form of EMR of the suns energy. In the Emerald Tablet which describes the "Operation of the Sun" it states that "This is the Greatest Force of all powers, because it overcomes every subtle thing and penetrates every solid thing".

All light from the Sun is not limited to the visible spectrum, for the light (EMR=electromagnetic radiation) of the Sun penetrates every solid thing. Just as x-rays can penetrate our flesh to visually see bone structure, so to do microwaves, gamma rays etc., penetrate much denser matter, nothing is solid.

The Sun is a physical manifestation of Higher Consciousness (of which we can physically see), Light is Illumination. And in Light there is information and knowledge. We are ourselves a manifestation constructed of Higher Intelligence. Everything is composed of energy and emits Light, though we only see the physical body with our eyes, given the right sight we could see even the light that is emitted from our own cellular construct.

We are all bodies of Light, and it is our Soul that is the individual manifestation, energy body of an evolving consciousness within the cosmic construct.

We are essentially composed of the Suns energy, Anima is the Source of Life. The Sun was worshipped widely by many in various Ancient civilizations. To the Egyptians the Sun was the most powerful God; for in it was the source of All life, energy and Light. It was not the worship of the Sun itself as a God, but in the quintessence of its inherent powers. It is the life giving power and energy of its source, which was highly revered by the Ancient Ones.

During those times they did not know its

scientific composition, they knew only of its essence to give Light and Life. However today, we may know that the Sun is largely made of hydrogen and helium and that it is a super mass of hot plasma, but this, by no means gives any real understanding of its true power.

The Sun we see is only a physical manifestation of something much greater that we cannot see. It is within the Realm of Anima that Consciousness becomes absorbed and infused by the Light. We all belong to Anima, Anima is the god/goddess of the Soular System, and it communicates with all consciousness within the Soular System. It is by his/her Light that we experience conscious evolution. Through Anima we are all connected, and it is through Anima that we are connected beyond the Soular System to other Soular Systems that have their own radiant Suns and stars.

Anima is the nucleic control center of our own Soular System, so too are billions of other star Suns the nucleic center of their own conscious evolution Soular System. And every star is connected via light waves, photon packets of information being transmitted between these stars and transferred from one Soular System to another over vast distances.

Each Soular System is connected by light waves of each Sun, reaching light years across space carrying with it knowledge and information across the cosmos, All of which are in constant contact and communicating with each other.

In its truest simplicity, connect the dots (each star sun) to reveal the structure that is of the highest cosmic order. And by so doing, does the multiverse take shape to reveal the construct of the universe.

As can be seen in the provided images, by connection and linking the Suns and stars does the universe begin to take on formation. It is a multi-verse of universes all connected by every point of light transferring information from one point to another, binding All things as One.

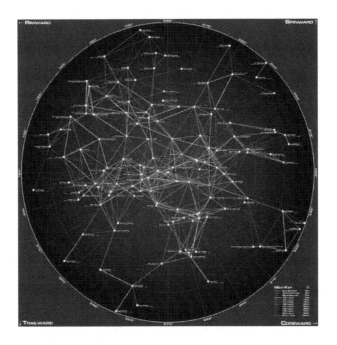

"We inhabit a universe where atoms are made in the centers of stars; where each second a thousand suns are born; where life is sparked by sunlight and lightning in the airs and waters of youthful planets; where the raw material for biological evolution is sometimes

made by the explosion of a star halfway across the Milky Way;

...where a thing as beautiful as a galaxy is formed a hundred billion times - a Cosmos of quasars and quarks, snowflakes and fireflies, where there may be black holes and other universe and extraterrestrial civilizations whose radio messages are at this moment reaching the Earth. How pallid by comparison are the pretensions of superstition and pseudoscience; how important it is for us to pursue and understand science, that characteristically human endeavor. "
Carl Sagan: COSMOS

Each star sun, is as unique as each individual creature. Though in structure we are much the same, each composed of identical materials and chemicals our consciousness is uniquely our own. It is the mind of each being that remains exclusively unique. For we are more than mere structural beings, we are energy beings, we are information within a larger construct.

Consciously connected. So too then is Anima

a physical structure of which we can see with our eyes, but there is an intellectual energy being beyond our senses that we cannot completely see. We only see the fiery spherical structure of a much more powerful illuminated manifestation.

The Sun is the source of life and intelligence within the Ordo Anima, it is in direct connection, with all that resides within its orbital force. However, it is also linked to all other nearby star/suns. The Suns and Stars of the universe are like a macrocosmic neural network of a supra-conscious higher intelligence. Information is transmitted from one Sun unto the others, each in constant contact via an invisible fiber optic like Light wave transmitting photonic particles, couriers of information. Indeed, all things are connected. We have access to knowledge billions of light years away, as our own consciousness becomes Illuminated do we come to know this connection better.

As alluded to earlier, Anima is the central intelligence center of our Solar System. Within it is the sacred knowledge and information that has fueled life on all planets and spheres of consciousness within its realm. Anima is the courier of a sacred Light whose rays of consciousness reach out to every planet within the Soular System and beyond to connect with other central suns of intellectual illumination.

Inevitably, we are a connected to Anima and we are a part of its journey through space. Alas, we cannot yes fathom infinity and the vastness of space. Everything is in motion. Anima itself is traveling through the cosmos at approximately 45,000 miles per hour/ 72,000 kilometers per hour. Our Soular System is not in a stationary orbit with each planet just circling the Sun, it is much more dynamic than that. The Sun is traveling through space with each planet spinning around it in a vortex as it shoots through space on an unknown journey through the cosmos.

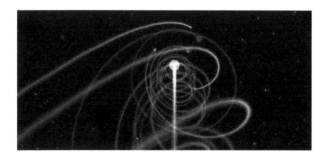

Understand, that the macrocosm is a reflection of the microcosm. Light carries information. Therefore, it is imperative that you understand the importance of your own Light. For you yourself are a body of Light. You only see the physical manifestation, however, under new lenses we could witness the radiance of each and every soul on this planet.

Just as the billions of neurons are firing through your own brain as you are reading this, carrying and processing information through an amazing universe within your own consciousness, so too is Anima traveling through the mind of a higher consciousness of which we are directly connected to.

As mentioned earlier, the Sun has long been worshiped as a God, it has been referenced as a God of Light. It has had a long following of ancient civilizations that have reisen to great hieghts and fell to extinction. It is not here that we advocate the revisitation of Sun worship, it is here that we advocate the awareness of Anima as a fire of the Soul, your own Soular Consciousness and that within all others.

Anima, our Sun, is the Lake of Fire spoke of in certain ancient texts, for billions of years, eternally burning. However, it is not an everlasting damnation for the torment of souls, it is an inferno of Divine Light and Consciousness.

It is the "Operation of the Sun", indeed shall you be consumed by it, for that is the nature of the cosmos. As Above, So Below! Just as the ant hill has its queen, and the hive has its queen, with drones, scouts etc., so to does Anima have her servants to the Soular System.

And As Above, So Below, so too does Anima feed off energies and consciousness. Anima is of Love and Light, but it is also of consuming and devouring energies to survive. Anima feeds off energies, and one day you too will be consumed and infused by it. This is the Way. Energy does not die, it is transformed, so too shall you be transformed.

Here shall we include an ancient text known as the Emerald Tablet, The Operation of the Sun. Herein shall you come to know the inner workings of Cosmic Consciousness, Conscious Evolution and Transformation.

The Emerald Tablet

In Truth without Deceit, certain and most Veritable.

That which is Below, corresponds to that which is Above, and that which is Above corresponds to that which is Below, to accomplish the miracles of the One Thing. Through the meditation of One Mind, so do all created things originate from One Thing, through Transformation.

It's Father is the Sun, its Mother is the Moon. The Wind carries it in its Belly; its Nurse is the Earth. It is the Origin of All, the consecration of the Universe, its inherent strength is Perfected, if it is turned into Earth.

Separate the Earth from Fire, the Subtle from the Gross, gently with great Ingenuity. It rises from the Earth to Heaven and descends again to Earth, thereby combining within Itself the Powers of both the Above and Below.

Thus, will you obtain the Glory of the Whole Universe. All Obscurity will be clear to you. This is the Greatest Force of All Powers, because it overcomes every Subtle thing and penetrates every Solid Thing.

In this way was the Universe Created. From this comes many wonderous Applications, as this is the Pattern.

Therefore, I am called Thrice Greatest Hermes, having all three parts of the Wisdom of the Whole Universe. Herein have I completely explained the Operation of the Sun.

The Cosmic Construct
Cosmic Consciousness

Though Anima is a massive star of which our tiny planet has taken up orbit and by so doing has utilized the energy of the sun to propagate life as we know it today, in the vastness of the cosmos we must be aware of how minute we really are. However, we must also be very conscious of the fact that we are not irrelevant in the grand scheme of things.

Quantum physics states that everything is energy, pure energy. Therefore it would be safe to assume that in quantum metaphysics everything is consciousness, and even more true, everything is pure consciousness. To implicate that the hermetic saying "That which is Above corresponds to that which is Below" has great gravity when we come to understand that the macrocosm is a reflection of the microcosm.

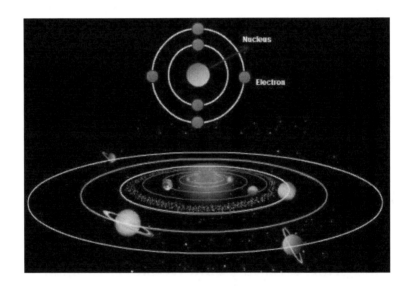

For by comparison, the Soular System resembles an atomic structure. Both containing a central nucleus center.

A galaxy spiraling resembles a cellular structure also containing a nucleic center which is composed of a massive star cluster. Therefore much like the Soular System, the galaxy itself has a centralized collective core intelligenceThe vastness of the universe contains billions of galaxies all of which are flowing through the fluidic infinite abyss of a vast cosmic consciousness.

Everything is in motion, everything is energy, and everything is pure consciousness. The billions of galaxies are as cells flowing through the construct of the universe, all connected and held true by an unseen force of Light.

Everything arises from the mind, the mind creates everything. And as it is, this same mind force resides in all of us. In all things. The mind is pure energy, and even though you are a minute manifestation in an infinite abyss, the mind force is present within you, and has great power within you. So much so, that your own brain cells reflect the universe itself.

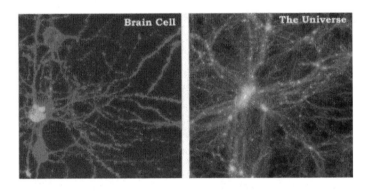

Brain Cell · The Universe

All things unify into a fractal universe that is the Absolute, the One Mind. The secret of creation, the secret of manifestation is All is Mind; it is the Mind of All. Therefore, everything originated in the Mind. If one were to ask one self, from whence do thoughts arise? One can without a doubt, state it is unknown. Are our thoughts truly our own thoughts or perhaps the thoughts of something of Higher Intelligence. More of a neural network of billions of minds sharing information and knowledge, and acting as one.

Einstein's theory of relativity stated that nothing could travel faster than the speed of light. However, if All is Mind then perhaps thought may be the fastest thing in the universe. For everything is traveling at the speed of thought. This does not reference information, as information is carried through Light, photon packets. The Mind is more than information, it is thought. Per se, if asked to think of the Sun, your mind can process this much faster than light from the Sun can travel to Earth (~ 8 mins). The mind can process information much faster than light can travel.

All is Mind, All is connected, All is within you.

Collectively, all consciousness is of the Cosmic Consciousness, the Mind of God. A God Mind that encompasses all thought and this in no way insinuates one singularity of a particular religion. Anima is the Lord of Light of this Soular System. Anima is like a neuron traveling through the All, transporting our own Planetary Consciousness with it throughout the universe. And the universe itself also traveling through the One Mind carrying Anima with it.

What is known, that given this perception of the One Mind, our kind can see through the Light of their own mind into the Mind of All. We have, through the access of our own consciousness, contact with the Cosmic Consciousness. And thereby can we be influential in creation and the manifestation of one's own purpose. It has been said that each and every one of us are a star. A child of God. Stars shine and children grow up. There comes a time when we must grow up in the image of our Creator and shine bright of our own radiance. It is then that we come into our own power to create reality.

The power of God, the One Mind, the Cosmic Consciousness is inherent within us. It is our calling to come into the Light of Anima, infuse the Intellectual Illumination of Anima into our own consciousness deliberately seeking the Light.

As Above, So Below! All is but a fractal, patterns upon like pattern replicating itself billions of times over billions of light years. Layer upon layer, upon layer. Each layer building upon the other, again and again, replicating itself like the division of one cell into two identical cells, two into four, into eight, into sixteen, into thirty two, into sixty four... ad infinitum.

Chaos is an Order yet to be Deciphered

The Cosmic Structure is built upon a copulation of chaos and order. There is a pattern to everything, though we may decide through our own limited perceptions and lack of understanding that that which seems to have not a pattern must be chaos, when in actuality it is a coming order of its own accord. To know, in order for there to be a New Order, that which currently exist must be deconstructed. The end is only the beginning of something new.

For we must know that in destruction doeth give rise to new construction. Energy does not die, it is transformed. Our consciousness will never die, it will be transformed. It has done so on various levels through the Soulificati.

We are a small part of a vast consciousness, small but not irrelevant nor powerless. For we have the power to effect reality. It is all in the Mind. There is a degree of thought form, that has the power and ability to shape reality, to foresee that which is to come. Visionary thought, close your eyes that you may see, do not be disillusioned by the illusions. The world around you appears solid, yet there is space and energy even in the most solid of structures.

The power to alter reality exists already within each and every one you. The more one masters each level of consciousness, the closer one comes to activating their own Higher Consciousness and thereby becoming more and more influential in the Cosmic Construct of the Mind of All.

Chapter XIII

Conclusion

Questions lead to answers which should always lead to more questions, and even more profound answers. Question everything, that you may find the answers you seek. Within the book of the Soulificati, you peered through the veil of various levels of consciousness, and expanded your own consciousness by so doing. Where you take it from here will be of your own design and intent. The information herein is designed to expand your own consciousness and intellectual illumination.

Within you, and all, is the power to shape reality. Everything is energy, everything is Mind. Our minds have the capacity to shape reality and to manifest our own desires and intent. Heighten your energy by absorbing the Light of Anima, know that when you eat, be it plant or animal, you are absorbing the energy of Anima as that which you ingest, ingested the same source for its own sustainment.

By connecting to the Light of Consciousness do we thereby connect to the One Mind. Visualize the connection of Light between all other minds with ones own, then all those minds including yours, connected to Anima. And then Animas to every other star/sun in the galaxy, then every galaxy connected forming the neural network that is the Cosmic Construct, which is the One Mind of All things.

As stated many times, That which is Above is as That which is Below, and That which is Below is as that which is Above. All of which is a reflection of ones own brain, neural network and mind. You whole body is a conscious construct, not just the brain. The neural network is connected through the whole body through the nervous system. Communicate, sense, feel, listen, receive and transmit, and radiate the sacred knowledge encoded within you.

The silent voice within. Heed that guidance that is within you and around you. The Keepers will guide you when you are ready to transcend. Take heed to all minds in which you connect with, as the Keepers communicate through us all and all things. Trust in the universe, but most importantly trust in thyself. For we are indeed a reflection of the universe itself, the microcosm and macrocosm are one.

Herein have we imparted a vision of the Highest Order, assimilate it into your own consciousness. See how every level of consciousness is inclusive to ones own consciousness, and how it all is layer upon layers of consciousness that is pure.

Know that within you is a force of unconsciousness, a primordial force of potentiality. A part of yourself that is not yet awakened. From this dawns the subconscious. The subconscious is an abyss of unstructured information, flashes of insight, random knowledge, visions of possibilities, dreams and untapped resources. Focus on that which you want, that which you know within you is to be that which is your Higher Self. From the depths of the subconscious shall come visions of greatness.

From the subconscious, comes consciousness. There is motivation to act, to do, and inspiration to become. This base level of consciousness is not self aware, until it reaches the next level and comes to the revelation that it exist.

This revelation itself, possess its own diversity of multiple layers. For one to realize they exist at the base level is to fight for survival, to avoid the termination of ones life. At the next level, it seeks to gratify itself with acquisitions of identity and then at the highest level it realizes it has a purpose and endeavors to live with purpose. And then at this level does it commit to an even higher purpose.

Indeed, we can look around us and see the brutality of selfish people, fighting and crying to be recognized as important. Working their life away for money, status and prestige. Then we see others who are purpose driven to make a change in the world, succeeding not to only better their life, but the lives of others.

Prior to this level of conscious evolution, there must exist a level of conformity that recognizes structures and patterns in all things. To abide by the rules before we can break them, change them and/or supersede them.

Once we have successfully spent our time conforming to the norms and understanding the dynamics of mediocrity, our self awareness realizes that it has the inherent power to make things happen, with our hands as well as with our minds. It is then that we begin to shape our own reality. We can see that through our physical efforts do we possess the power to shape the world in which we exist.

It is here then we must learn to be assertive, to stand up for what we want and what we believe. Before peace comes war. We have to find within our self that warrior, that driving force that is dynamic, powerful and assertive. When this has been mastered we come to a place where we need to master balance and to do so must find and cultivate peace within our self and in others. There is a constant conflict within ourselves, for at this level of being is our physical dimension dualistic. The greatest and most victorious of battles, are the ones fought within our self.

Once we find a certain level of peace within, we can come to know and understand the higher power of love. We connect in ways that are enigmatic. Shaping connections with ourselves, with others and with the universe. Reality responds to us more accordingly and within we feel a love of all things. Within this level of Love, there is a purity of purpose an inner knowing.

This knowing, this love of all things, knows that hate is an amplification of love threatened. We must fight for what we love, but we should not harbor the negativity of a consuming hate.

With this level of love we are compelled to share this passion and love with others. This may be on a business level where we share our passion for a product or service, on a mental level where we are passionate about our beliefs and on a spiritual level where we live our lives to our highest ideal and purpose passionately.

On a more metaphysical dimension, this level of consciousness serves as a messenger. It has been imbued with a purpose and Light that has become infused with Anima. It has reached a level of frequency that is closely aligned with Anima. It continues to become brighter, more radiant and illuminated.

Once aligned with, and one with Anima, consciousness is Illuminated. Thereby attaining the capacity to communicate at higher frequencies and travel at the speed of thought through the Soular System or via the light waves between all Soular Systems.

As mentioned earlier, the light waves between Suns/Stars are information viaducts of conscious transmissions. Providing a pattern, and in actuality a map that consciousness can travel throughout the Cosmic Construct. The human brain has over thirty billion neurons, and more synapses than there are stars in the Milky Way galaxy. The transmission of photon packets of Light carrying information from star system to star system are like neurotransmitters of our own brain. We are the neurotransmitters of consciousness within the Cosmic Construct. The Universe is continually developing and generating Higher Consciousness within all things, to include our own consciousness.

In conclusion, there is in all things a message. There exist information all around us. Everything has consciousness to a degree, you can tap into all consciousness through your own consciousness, as you already have access to it. You are already connected to this vast network of Higher and Lower frequencies of Consciousness.

Authors Notes:

UNCONSCIOUSNESS: This is not the absence of consciousness, the unconscious is not consciousness of itself, of others or its environment. It is strictly governed by impulse and influence of external stimuli. It is like the base operating system of a computer, the hidden codes and prompts. Unconsciousness within our own being controls ones breathing, ones heartbeat. If one is unconscious due to head trauma, the body can still breathe, and the heart can still beat of its own accord.

Unconscious is influenced by impulse, and it can be manipulated by external stimuli. Meaning it can be influenced by its external environment but is not aware of its environment. For example, to retreat from heat or from cold, to gravitate toward something that it is attracted to, or repulse from something it is not. It can be pricked and it will twitch. As mentioned, it is as the base operating system of a computer, it is an imbedded response mechanism. It impulsively provides the essentials behind the scenes so that the conscious being can focus on greater things. Therefore, it can be influenced positively or negatively and it will respond accordingly without awareness of why or how.

SUBCONSCIOUS: the subconscious is as an abyss of thoughts, images and ideas. It takes all experiential data and constantly assimilates and dis-assimilates information. It is as a vast library of information, unorganized, yet it can locate information seamlessly and with great ingenuity.

Though the information may appear to be chaotic and random, the subconscious can be tapped into to attain powerful visions, hidden knowledge and secrets that can aide and abide one in their endeavors. The mind assimilates the vast knowledge based on the entities experiences and needs. And thereby can deliver to one, that which it seeks to know and can also give sight of ones vision and purpose in life.

There are ways in which one can more readily tap into this vast resource of knowledge through hypnosis and meditations that alter the brainwaves from Beta, to Alpha to Delta and Theta.

Ask of it to bring to you to the surface, that

which you need to fulfill your purpose, and/or even develop a lifes mission if not already present. The subconscious is deeply connected to intuition. Trust your intuition, trust the inner knowing. Be that which you were designed to be. The knowledge and power are present within the All, and your mind is connect to this vast resource of information.

As mentioned, the subconscious is a vast resource that stores all information from all consciousness, to include your own and that of all others. It is the dream pool of Cosmic Consciousness. Within it are stored all potentialities, yet can only be accessed at the depths of ones own design.

CONSCIOUSNESS: The base level of consciousness within the Soulificati, becomes aware of its environment and its surrounding. It is aware of everything around it in relation to itself, yet it is not aware of itself. It follows without question what it is designed to do, not so much through conformity yet, but because it knows no other way.

Every cell in your body is a conscious entity, it holds fast to its obligation with an unwavering servitude. Plants are conscious, yet their degree of self awareness is undetermined exactly. What is evident is that they are aware of the environment around them; such as sunlight, darkness, water, drought, fire, and even the vibrations of other plants and animals around them. However, noting here this is not to say a plant is not self aware, some research conducted demonstrates otherwise. This was only an example of the degree of base consciousness. As some research conducted on plants can possibly verify a plant can sense a threat to itself.

This simply demonstrates that consciousness at this level is already encoded with a sense of self preservation, yet it is not essentially self aware to the extent that it knows it is a plant. Therefore this level of conscious manifestation is driven to survive on the premises that it needs to, not knowing why, only that it must continue to exist and do what it does as designed. At this level it is not so much of self-importance as it is self preservation strictly out of necessity.

CONSCIOUS CONFORMITY: All animals, including humans are subjected to conscious conformity at an early age. Insects are more of the previous conscious level of existing without knowing why, they are simply driven by their instincts to do what they are designed to do. They do not act out, they do not play nor do they question their design. However, higher levels of consciousness require conditioning and discipline to program the consciousness to comply with the clan and cultural expectations for its own survival, and the survival as a whole.

Conformity defined is a compliance with standards, rules or laws. Also, it is defined as a behavior in accordance with socially accepted conventions or standards. The process of conformity is typically mandated and upheld through some form of punishment if one does not comply.

For the human species specifically, children initially cry for what they need or want but as they grow older they are taught manners and proper conduct of communicating their needs and wants. They are taught to behave a certain way that is deemed acceptable by a social normality. There are two types of people that would be noteworthy to take heed of in regards to conformity. One being the people who seek to control by always forcing standards, rules and laws upon others to keep people below them or in check. The others are the people who are fearful and comply without question, placing all their faith in the system. The faithful and unquestioning follower.

It would behoove thee, to be compliant to the laws of the land. However, as ones consciousness ascends, the only one true law within the Soular System and that is the will of Anima. It is advisable to conform to a degree that one is not incarcerated or terminated, however, never allow any social acceptance dictate your transcendence. Conformity has its place, it is to protect more than ones self, it is to protect the group.

Conformity instills higher standards, moral conduct and decency depending on the mindset of the group. In the coming level of consciousness, it can be brutal where violence is the standard of savage behavior and socially acceptable.

This is within the nature of the Order, but remember to ascend one must transcend. Inevitably, One should only conform to that which one holds true to their heart and soul, for some forms of conformity can and will imprison the mind and soul, and dim ones light.

SELF AWARENESS: when conscious

become self aware, it reaches a new level of manifestation. It is safe to say that most humans are self aware at a base level. They know when they are hungry or thirsty, they eat and drink. When they are hot or cold they dress appropriately. The level that separates them is to what degree that they satisfy these basic needs. What they eat and how they dress distinguishes them from instinctual beasts.

This level of consciousness is all about ones self, especially in relation to others. At this base level of self awareness, it wants to be important, it wants to be desired and wanted by others, it wants to belong. On the opposite side of the spectrum, it may not uphold a good outlook about itself and have a low self esteem. It may not stay healthy through its eating habits, it may not care for its hygiene properly, and its overall appearance is dross.

Self Aware beings naturally group with other like minded Self Aware beings. This is a natural inclination of survival in numbers. However, the collaboration of like minds builds packs, clans, tribes, organizations, civilizations and even Empires.

It is within such structures that the individual

seeks its own identity, its place, metaphorically within the greater scheme of things. It seeks to belong. Within such structures individual intelligence becomes a part of something greater than itself, playing its part knowingly. It is here that Self Awareness, still very closely imbedded with the Conformity Conscious, works to shape reality, but not necessarily of its own design but the design of another Higher Level Conscious, per se that of a Ruler.

The Ruler Conscious is above the consciousness of others in that it has a vision and most importantly is either aggressive or assertive in its conduct.

This level of Self Awareness typically is aware of its self and its needs yet has not become assertive enough to transcend to higher levels of manifestation.

ASSERTIVE CONSCIOUSNESS: It is when consciousness is Self Aware and becomes assertive that it begins to challenge others and its own Conformity Conscious to get what it wants. As you go through life, take notice of those who are assertive and those who are not. It is easy to see in their demeanor and actions. Those who are assertive get things done and do it well, they even get others to get things done for them. They have a drive, and are very motivated to their cause, be it a selfish cause or a cause for the greater good.

We can group within this level of consciousness the a degree of aggression, as aggression is a amped up form of assertiveness that is less positive. However, it can get ones intent manifested as well. Aggression is more warlike more conflictual as it is more hostile and violent. Aggression accomplishes out of fear where assertiveness accomplish out of respect and mutual benefit.

Take heed to those who are assertive and those who are aggressive. An aggressive conscious can be hostile and violent whereas an assertive consciousness is more confident and forceful. One must develop this level of conscious accordingly as the aggressor will be combative, the assertor will be more persuasive and forceful without conflict where possible.

As consciousness become Higher and Higher, it develops its own forceful presence. It can ascend in either state as warlike and violent or it can ascend in its own confidence and inner peace to find a balance. Noting that even though a combative consciousness can ascend to the higher levels, this force will fight for its cause until its death, whereas a confident conscious may not.

It is imperative to integrate both a warlike nature as well as a forceful presence that is confident in its true self. For as one ascends to higher level's it must possess within itself a strength to stand strong for that which it believes in and loves, it must fight for its cause, its purpose.

This is not limited to a strength of body in as much as it is a strength of spirit that separates one from all others. In a warlike nature, the true battle is within, to transcend and overcome one current state of being and ascend to the highest level of consciousness, Illumination.

BALANCED CONSCIOUSNESS: at this level of consciousness, there is an inner turmoil, and unsettled experience of consciousness, pulling one to seek peace within. It exists in a dualistic nature. It experiences moments of turmoil and moments of peace. It comes to know the pain and the pleasure. It is driven by one or the other.

Herein the Soulificati, this is where our current consciousness currently reside, hanging in the balance of love and war, good and bad, right and wrong, pain and pleasure, peace and war.

The human brain itself is separated into two hemispheres of creativity and logic, imagination and analysis, feelings and facts, visualization and language, holistic and details, Spirituality and organization. In order to ascend one must become integrated in their thinking capacity by harnessing and mastering both sides of their brain. Understand that thinking is not limited to the brain alone, the whole body is itself in totality a unified thinking organism. The brain is like a processor but the whole nervous system connects the entire body in thought.

The Egyptians believed that the Solar Plexus was the seat of all thought. That thought arose from the heart region. The Hermetics attribute the brain to intelligence, the King; and the heart to intuition, the Queen. The marriage (conjoining) of which gave birth to the Hermaphrodite child, the god child.

It is evident in our current realm on Earth, most people are imbalanced and without inner peace. The King and Queen battling each other, and working against each other, and even divorced from each other. This imbalance will cause one to be either overly logical or overly emotional. Logic (intelligence) is the acquisition of knowledge externally, whereas emotions (intuition) are the acquisition of knowledge internally.

Emotions are energy in motion within oneself. Such emotions are caused by external stimuli of a higher degree. Others actions, experiences and thoughts stimulated externally influence ones emotions, positively or negatively. For example, the death of someone can cause sorrow, ones companion being unfaithful can cause jealousy, hate and/or anger. The weather can make one depressed. Ones loneliness can cause sadness. The emotions and intuition are closely connected, as external stimuli can also cause gut feelings of what is going on, or what is going to happen. The intuition processes information at a deeper level.

A component of intuition is an inner knowing, knowing something without having logic to support the knowing. On higher developed consciousness the intuition and intelligence are integrated and work in unison to further ascend Higher Consciousness within ones self and within others.

Find the balance, find a sense of inner peace within yourself that you may overcome the turmoil and anguish of matters that no longer advance your being to higher states of becoming. With an inner sense of knowing and an inner sense of peace, one can remain steadfast and unmoved in ones purpose.

LOVE CONSCIOUSNESS: As with all levels of consciousness, Love has many levels. There is a love one feels for their parents, their siblings, their children, their friends, their partners, their job, their favorite places and foods, their belongings, their environment, their world, their ideals, their God, their Spirit and their Universe. Each carries with it a varying degree of Love.

To love, is not to be weak. Indeed, it can make us seem weak in that we may put others before us, we may even endure hardships to help the ones we love, we may sacrifice our own needs for the needs of the ones we love. At this level this is a sense of duty to our tribe, family, culture or companions.

However, this is not weakness, it takes great strength to sacrifice ones self and ones needs for another.

Many of us have been hurt by the ones we love/d, and in this pain we have built a wall around ourselves to protect us from further pain. Enduring pain makes one stronger, hiding and protecting oneself from further pain is weakness. The hardships of menial love prepares us for Higher Love. Indeed the head will over-rule the heart to protect it from possible pain in the future. A natural survival response is to protect our self from perceived threats. Either one will hide in fear or one will become confrontational and combative to ward off perceived potential threats.

It is apparent in most all relationships that people carry with them baggage from previous relationships. Carrying that baggage around weakens the body, mind and soul. And it has the potential to destroy future relationships. It takes great strength to drop the baggage and open up to love again after we have been hurt. No one said this would be easy. Yes, it is wise to learn from the past, however, it is unwise to carry it's weight into the future.

Most all of us have been hurt by love in one way or another, yet it is of Higher Consciousness to continue to love and to love without conditions. To open up to the Higher Consciousness of Love means to find within ones own self, a Self Love. One cannot love without loving ones self. Accept who you are and accept that everything that has happened to you thus far has created the person you are. If you are not happy with yourself, seek out the reason why, and fix it.

Therefore, love without inhibitions, find a lust for life, a passion for all life and a love of Self. Come to know the inherent powers of the universe within your Self, sense it and feel it moving through you. Love is not weakness. Pure love is power, it is the union, the integration of ones self with the Source of All things. You are of your own universe with the power to connect with all things at all levels.

Let go of anger and hate, it is harmful energy that depletes your light. Accept all that has transpired thus far has brought you to who you are now. Listen to that which is within you, there is a passion dying to create, to become and to exist. In all that you do, do so with an unwavering love and passion. When one reaches the Highest Conscious level of Love, then and only then is one Self Sovereign and the master of thy Self.

MESSENGER CONSCIOUS: as one continues to master their own consciousness and understand it, so too can they understand it within others. When you have reached a level of inner peace and transcended through love, the message you carry encrypted within you becomes ones passion. There is no stopping the love and light that radiates within your soul.

As a messenger one possesses the ability to communicate at all levels of consciousness to a degree, for one has connected with all things. Everything is energy and everything is information being transmitted and received. At this level, one is tuned in to all frequencies of broadcasted information.

In daily applications of a Messenger Conscious within this realm, we possess the power to communicate at various levels naturally and reach people in profound ways. Not doing so for personal gain, and not doing so to control or harm.

At this level, transcendent through love, this source of communication is to the benefit of all involved.

The message we bring will not always be well accepted, however, through communication at this level, seeds are planted in the minds of others. They will take root in time and alter consciousness contacted. If it is that you find yourself delivering your message and it is to control another, harm another or toward your own advancement, know that this is a key indicator you are not communicating at a Soular level and remain in a lower frequency of information. The Messenger does not seek to manipulate or control, the message carried by a Messenger Conscious, is a powerful influence of its own source. It is delivered, shared and transmitted out of Love.

Per se, this book that you are reading now, is delivering a message to your own conscious evolution. It is delivered in such a manner that influences your consciousness, and not to manipulate it or control it. It is delivered with a sincere love of all who come in contact with this information. It does not instruct you, it is designed to influence your thinking in such a way that any and all choices made will inevitably be your own.

The Messenger Conscious delivers the message, what the recipient does with the knowledge remains their own decision.

Spiritually, the Messenger speaks within ones own self, there is a Messenger within you, your own Messenger Consciousness ascending. There are also Messengers in others, as well as Messengers without a physical body are present. Messenger Conscious is highly advanced and is closely connected with the Illuminated One. We are all connected with the Illuminated One, but the Messengers possess the source of Light of the Highest Order.

ILLUMINATED CONSCIOUSNESS: Illumination is the Light of the Mind, it is the Source of All things. It is the Light of Consciousness and the Source of All Knowing. It is a radiant flame of the Soul, and the Soul is a body of Light. An Illuminated Mind within a human form, is very rare but not impossible. For this level of consciousness has access to knowledge that is literally out of this world.

There is a powerful presence that radiates from this state of being. It has the power to touch souls in ways that greatly influence transcendence and ascension. It communicates on all levels of consciousness, its Light of Illumination penetrates the dross and purifies all energies.

The Illuminated Consciousness is connected to all other conscious beings, near and far. It can communicate with other consciousness light years away. It does not have to wait for the answer, it already has the answer. For example, a seeker may ask an Illuminated Being a question, this question triggers a specific frequency within the Mind of the Illuminated One, and the answer is instantly brought to Light. The Illuminated Mind does not have to commit anything to memory, for the information is already there and will always be there for all who can access the Source. The processing speed of information through the Source is infinitely instantaneous.

Illuminated consciousness is omniscient, omnipresent and omnipotent. It is encrypted and present in every light bearing source. Your own body radiates energy which is of itself a Bringer of Light. Just was the Sun itself radiates and illuminates consciousness on all levels, so too does the Illuminated Consciousness exist beyond space and time and is infinite.

In closing, we only ask that you consider the implications of conscious evolution as disclosed herein. That you give a sincere effort toward understanding the Construct of Cosmic Consciousness and of thy own conscious evolution. By so doing may you access the knowledge of where thoughts arise and whose thoughts they are. Are they truly your own thoughts? Or are you accessing the Source? Only you will come to know the answer to this for yourself in time.

As there have been times where you have deliberately sought an answer to some perplexing question, and miraculously the answer revealed itself to you. From whence did this knowledge come? Seek to know the Source of Illumination, for you are one of us, the Soulificati. You may exist within this current realm of manifestation, however, you are something much more, something much greater than your physical form. For you are connected to the Source and thereby have access to the consciousness of All things.

LUX PRINCIPIUM

SCIENTIA ENIM VIRTUS, COGNOSCO DEBEAS

ADEPTUS AD LUCEM

Made in the USA
Columbia, SC
20 June 2020